Praise fo

"This book is chock-full of solid practical *and* spiritual advice on so many topics. Church renewal, leadership development, conflict management and resolution, discipleship practices, strategic planning, multi-siting—these are just some of the ways Douglas A. Hill serves readers of his book. Doug's writing about his work at Abiding Hope gives us *all* hope that congregational revitalization is achievable."
—**Reggie McNeal**, city coach at GoodCities, church leadership consultant, author of *Missional Renaissance* and *Kingdom Come*

"Written with hard-won wisdom and humility, this book offers excellent practical guidance for the development of anchor churches and partner congregations, for leadership development that fosters revitalization, and for creating the kind of ministry teams that can work with the pastor to generate lively and fruitful ministry in any size church. Douglas A. Hill's writing is winsome and accessible, while grounded in solid research."
—**Elaine A. Heath**, retired dean, Duke University, author, speaker, consult, and president of Neighborhood Seminary

"In a time when countless congregations and their leaders are trying to find their way towards vitality, here comes a book written by a theologically savvy experienced pastor with a road map that works. Undergirded with a no-nonsense ache for renewal of God's mission in the world and a love for the church, this book promises to bring about hope and a renewal of call for pastors and congregational leaders alike. Thank you, Pastor Doug Hill!"

—**Rick Barger**, leadership coach and consultant, retired pastor and seminary president, and author of *A New and Right Spirit: Creating an Authentic Church in a Consumer Culture*

"At last, a seasoned, battle-tested pastor with a heart for vitalized congregations has brought his insight, experience, and passion to bear on the most critical issue facing faith communities today: how to shift organizational culture. Like no other author I know, Douglas A. Hill weaves together a solid Biblical rationale, global and site-based organizational intelligence, and refreshing walk-the-talk honesty in this comprehensive, practical, and confidence-inspiring guide to developing a church culture that can nourish abundance while holding in check the toxins that are debilitating so many churches. He effectively advocates for replicable processes and best practices without falling prey to the one-size-fits-one prescriptions that set other leaders up to fail. Every turn of the pages in this book reveals practical pearls of wisdom laid in a setting of compassion and yearning found only in a pastor's heart. Take up and read."

—**J. Russell Crabtree**, author and founder of Holy Cow Consulting

"Douglas A. Hill writes for leaders weary of church *growth* language and shifts the focus to building cultures that enable church *life*. Written for pastoral leaders in the twenty-first century who Hill envisions as the architects of these cultures, the book serves as a blueprint for vitality to guide the courageous into the future God intends for all."

—**Brad A. Binau**, professor of pastoral theology and former academic dean, Trinity Lutheran Seminary at Capital University

"After personally working with Rev. Douglas A. Hill as a guide to create relationships and not programs within the congregation, I'm excited that his book will provide an opportunity for other leaders to participate in congregational cultural change. His book gives us a path to become change agents for the sake of God's mission; and through his book, he offers to walk alongside you as a conversation partner."

—Becky Piper, co-pastor of Calvary Lutheran Church, Rapid City, SD, and Anchor Church ministry partner with Woyatan Lutheran Church

"The vitality of the congregation I serve has been transformed through the lived experience of *Cultural Architecture*'s hopeful vision of congregational partnership. A must-read if you are looking to be inspired by how the Spirit is continuing to empower faithful leaders and renew the mission of the church today."

—Joel Rothe, Pastor, Christ the King Lutheran Church, Denver, CO

CULTURAL ARCHITECTURE

CULTURAL ARCHITECTURE

A PATH TO CREATING VITALIZED CONGREGATIONS

DOUGLAS A. HILL

Fortress Press

Minneapolis

CULTURAL ARCHITECTURE

A Path to Creating Vitalized Congregations

Print ISBN: 978-1-5064-6697-2

eBook ISBN: 978-1-5064-6698-9

Cover image: Abstract pattern / iStock / naqlewel

Cover design: Marti Naughton

For
Karrie, Sarah, and Jeremy

Contents

Introduction

It's *not* your fault.

—Reggie McNeal

With these words Reggie McNeal began his address in May 2018 to a group of lead pastors from the largest congregations in the Evangelical Lutheran Church in America (ELCA). Hearing those words from Reggie immediately moved me from my head to my heart. Instantly, I began to connect with my fatigue and frustration as a pastor, with the reality of how difficult parish ministry and leadership has become, with how most days I feel like I'm failing in my call and am unsure whether my leadership will lead to congregational vitality. Some of my colleagues around the room had even begun to weep. We all knew experientially what Reggie was saying.

It's not your fault that your congregations have been steadily declining over the past ten, twenty, thirty years.

It's not your fault that you are working harder than you've ever worked only to perpetually experience diminishing results.

It's not your fault that fewer and fewer people are attending worship and participating in ministry programs.

What made us pastors so emotional upon hearing Reggie's

words is that for years, even decades, we have carried the burden of congregational decline as though we were personally responsible. When you're the leader of the congregation called to bring the good news of the risen Christ to all the world, to make disciples of all nations, but you continually experience diminishing returns on ever greater investment, it's extraordinarily difficult (and perhaps impossible) not to take it personally. Men and women become pastors and professional church workers out of a deep love for God and the church. We have chosen the path of ministry to affect people's lives in positive ways—to make the world better through love, service, and generosity, and to help all people to live their true identity as children of God. And yet, over the past several decades the data tell us that we're failing. How are we not to take this personally?

Those of us in congregational leadership know all too well how the systems, methods, and practices that once served to promote congregational development no longer work. We've read the books, attended the workshops, engaged in the continuing education opportunities only to see little, if any, positive results. All mainline denominations report declining worship attendance and membership, as well as significant reductions in the number of people entering professional ministry. Even more staggering is the number of clergy who leave congregational ministry after only about five years of service. Let's not even talk about the increasing occurrences of substance abuse, divorce, and suicide among clergy. If you're reading this book, none of this is new information for you.

So, what are we to do? Let's start with confession. Let's confess, first of all, that many of us are ill-equipped to address the congregational challenges and struggles that exist today. The biblical and theological education that we received in seminary simply was not enough to prepare us for the reality of doing ministry in today's complex and rapidly changing context. Let's also confess that our denominational structures no longer provide the resources and support necessary to promote congregational vitality. Finally, we need to confess that we have largely operated an isolating congregational model in which each congregation attempts to be all things to all people with little, if any, collaboration with other congregations. Meeting once a week with other local pastors for text study or conducting an occasional joint worship service or participating in a shared Habitat for Humanity build are good things, but they are not enough to foster mutual development and bolster congregational health and vitality.

My intent is not to diminish such things; I'm simply stating that it's not enough. In spite of such shared activities, we often view neighboring congregations as competitors, built out of the mindset that the mission field is a zero-sum game with limited potential. Such thinking can even lead to the demonization of the few congregations that *are* vitalized and growing. Those serving struggling congregations may assume the few congregations that are vitalized have sold out to the evils of contemporary culture by catering to individualism and consumerism or by using secular tools such as marketing techniques or strategic development. While such condemning judgment may be accurate for some, I have found that it's not true for most vitalized congregations.

How much pain must we experience before we are ready to make a turn (dare I use the term *repent*) toward a new way, or perhaps an ancient way, of being church? When will we be humble enough to work together, I mean really work together, in creating a vibrant congregational identity and purpose that leads to vitality? Can we come together collectively to support one another in taking risks, knowing that many of our attempts will fail and yet also provide valuable information for charting new paths? Can we step outside our need for power and control, and instead trust the Spirit to guide us into places we've never gone? What would happen if we sought to learn from the best practices of healthy, vitalized congregations in order to create organic, relational networks beyond geographical judicatories? If these questions intrigue you, then keep reading. We're just getting started.

People, *Not* Programs

As we begin our exploration into congregational culture, we must ask ourselves, "What's our goal? What outcomes are we trying to produce?" Reggie McNeal (in the same keynote address referenced above) pointed out that the church has had the wrong focus or aim for quite some time. Our misguided focus has been on getting people into church. Think about the metrics we use to measure success: worship attendance, membership, and giving. Those are the primary numbers our judicatories want us to report. Those are the numbers our councils want to monitor. Those are the numbers we pastors ask each other to assess the other's ministries. By focusing on these numbers, it's easy to assume that our primary goal is to get people into church and to keep them there.

Reggie equates this thinking to a family going on vacation. To get where they desire to go (perhaps the beautiful Carolina coast), the family must first pass through an airport. If there's a storm or a situation with the aircraft, they get stuck there. Are they happy to be stuck in the airport? Of course not, because going to the airport and remaining in the airport is not their aim. The airport is simply a step in the chain of events necessary to arrive at their desired, true destination, the beach. Think of the church as the airport. The church is *not* the destination that people desire. No one comes to church just to be in church. They come to church searching for something more, searching for something deeper, searching for a greater destination. The church serves as a step in aiding people to arrive at their desired and true destination, which is *life* . . . full, whole, abundant life! (See John 10:10.) Somehow, we have forgotten or overlooked this simple reality. Furthermore, the process for generating abundant life is not to get people to attend programs or ministries, per se, but to immerse them in a culture, in a way of life that produces life. While such immersion might use certain programs or ministries (e.g., serving in the community, giving generously, participation in worship), the focus must always be on the development of people as they live into their true identity as children of God.

Have you ever experienced being asked or needing to ask someone to be the leader for a congregational program because no one else wanted to do it? Is the focus here on the person or the program? Clearly, the focus is on maintaining the program, and this is communicated indirectly, yet clearly, when a person is asked to serve in a role for which they are neither gifted nor passionate. How many people have been burned out by their church by being plugged into a committee simply because the constitution says that such a committee must exist? Or, how many people have been coerced into teaching Vacation Bible School or Sunday school because "We've always had these programs and someone needs to do it," even though no one wants to teach it or participate in it? The ability to shift away from maintaining programs toward generating an environment that cultivates abundant life for people requires astute cultural awareness and a high level of organizational intelligence. I call those who display such awareness cultural architects. Let's explore that phrase for a moment.

When Peter brings the news of the death and resurrection of Jesus and the inauguration of the new humanity to the people of Jerusalem, their first response is to ask, "What should we do?"[1] Peter's answer is simple, "Repent, and be baptized" (Acts 2:37–38). The Greek word *metanoia* literally means a "changed mind." Peter calls for the listeners to begin to see with new eyes, to think with new insights, to experience with new hearts. By calling them to the water, he calls them to be rebirthed into the new reality so that "there is a new creation: everything old has passed away; see, everything has become new!" (2 Cor 5:17). This movement from the old to the new is not a progressive experience of growing toward or moving into. Peter announces an end to the old and a radical birth of the new. There is no carryover from one to the next. We don't get to choose what we liked in the old and bring it with us into the new. It's a complete letting go, a dying, and a brand-new beginning, a rebirth.

This is the mindset that will best serve the church of twenty-first-century America as we go forward as the community of the new humanity. Many will want to cling to history and doctrine with the understanding that the church is gradually unfolding or in process or in discovery. But that's not the way God works. What we see in God is a perpetual cycle of deaths and resurrections through the flood narrative, to the call of Abraham and Sarah, to the crossing of the Jordan, to the sending of the Son. Early in Mark's Gospel, Jesus breaks the news to the Pharisees, saying, "No one puts new wine into old wineskins" (Mark 2:22). No matter how difficult such a message is for us to hear, it's a necessary call to die to the old and be rebirthed into the new.

A cultural architect is a person who has a clear understanding

---

1. For me, the term *new humanity* refers to the re-creation of all things through the resurrection of Christ. The death of Jesus represents the end of the old moral order governed by sin, division, hierarchy, and death. Saturday is an intentional gap or nothingness. Sunday is the new creation, new humanity, new moral order, governed by love and oneness with God, humanity, and the creation.

and assessment of the current toxic or ineffective culture, as well as a clear vision for the new culture to be created. The cultural architect must have the skills to articulate the new cultural vision and to create a strategic direction for living into that new culture. The cultural architect identifies and invests in key leaders to equip others for living into the new culture. The cultural architect ensures that all within the congregation align with the new culture.

The most difficult role of the cultural architect is keeping a hand to the plow and not looking back. Examples of cultural transformation within Scripture remind us that pushback, strong pushback, regarding the cultural transformation is very likely. People will cry out to go back to Egypt. They will deceive themselves into believing that the old ways were better. They will seek to avoid pain, just as Peter does when he challenges Jesus about going to Jerusalem, where he will be crucified. People will want to remain on mountaintops instead of being called into the valleys. The role of the cultural architect is not to get distracted by the cries of the people or the resistance to change, but to point continually to the new culture and lead the congregation toward the new vision.

This is not easy work. It will not happen without wounds, anguish, anxiety, and fear. This is the point at which many pastors get stuck because they have a difficult time handling the pain or anger of people resistant to change. The cultural architect must possess the emotional, relational, and organizational intelligence necessary to withstand the storms that occur during transformation, or the entire process will be derailed, and the congregation will find itself in a more precarious position than before the process began.

Unfortunately, I wasn't taught such things in seminary. Nor were the countless colleagues I've encountered throughout my twenty-five years of ordained ministry. Please don't misunderstand; I'm not being critical of seminaries. It's that I have found that organizational intelligence and cultural awareness cannot be taught in a classroom or captured fully in a book. In fact, I recognize that simply reading this book will not result in creating master cultural architects. There must be an applied context coupled with some form of ongoing coaching or mentoring to help shape people into effective leaders. There is no substitute for working contextually with a mentor or coach who uses organizational intelligence and cultural awareness within their role.

I am an advocate for residential theological education, as I have found that living in community while engaging in theological study can be an integral tool in forming cultural architects, as long as the community leaders are intentional about it. Beyond engaging in coursework, the student-in-residence has an opportunity to be immersed in a culture of faculty, administration, and peers living shared values that play an integral role in the students' formation. However, it's the contextualized internship experience that affords the student the opportunity to explore and experiment with organizational intelligence and cultural awareness. In my experience, a one-year internship is not enough time to form a student into a cultural architect. Trinity Lutheran Seminary in Columbus, Ohio, has adapted its curriculum for the master of divinity track to a two-plus-two system in which students spend their first two years in residential theological education, followed by two years of contextual education within a vitalized congregational setting, supervised by a cultural architect. Trinity's revised curriculum shows great potential for creating the needed cultural architects of the future.

Other systems and practices of judicatories have also fallen short in forming cultural architects and generating vitalized congregations. Having a single congregational-vitality staff person on a judicatory staff who is called to relate to umpteen pastors isn't enough. Sending pastors to annual leadership conferences isn't enough. The good news is that we don't have to throw the baby out with the bathwater and start from scratch. We can continue some of our current practices while also exploring new relational processes by which to connect, form, and develop cultural architects. To be sure, this sounds easier than it is, but if we work together to identify mentors and coaches and to connect them with pastors of high potential to help those pastors become more skilled in cultural development, we can get where God needs us to go.

Why Cultural Architects?

So, why this need for cultural architects? A powerful quotation often attributed to Peter Drucker (but not found in any of the thirty-nine books that he wrote) states: "Culture eats strategy for breakfast." A vitalized congregation, much like a vitalized family or a vitalized community, is all about culture. I define *culture* as "an environment conducive to developing life." When I'm sick and go to the doctor and she wants to confirm a diagnosis, often she will take a blood or fluid sample that will be "cultured" in the lab. Basically, the sample will be put into a contained, sterile environment to see what sort of bacteria or microbe grows or develops. All of us dwell in a blend of cultures that shape and form our identities. This, in turn, affects the choices and decisions we make for our lives. Our families, schools, workplaces, neighborhoods, and congregations all immerse us in cultures that influence our development as people and play a role in the lives that we live.

It's been said that a fish is unaware of the water in which it swims as a metaphor for humans often being unaware of the culture in which we subsist. A child growing up in an abusive home is often largely unaware that such a culture is abnormal or unhealthy. Just as a fish may be unaware of the effects that toxins in the water may have on its health or development, humans may be unaware of the effects a toxic culture at school or in a workplace or even in a congregation may have on their personal development. Becoming culturally aware is as difficult as becoming self-aware. I certainly have not enjoyed the times that I've been forced to look in the mirror, to face my own demons, to take a hard look at what Carl Jung would call "the Shadow." I much prefer to remain largely ignorant about such things, to avoid them at all costs, and even to distract or soothe myself through a plethora of self-medicating behaviors. However, lack of self-awareness and avoidance of the Shadow often results in self-defeating and relationship-defeating behaviors that prove to be destructive.

Becoming culturally aware presents similar challenges. That's probably why, instead of taking a deep, hard look at the toxicities present within a congregation that may be prohibiting development or vitalization, leaders often choose the path of creating new programs. For instance, several years ago we transformed Sunday school from individual, grade-based classes to a more Vacation Bible School–style experience, where kids of all ages joined together in the gym for games, music, crafts, and a short Bible lesson. Our leaders were surprised to discover that Bible Explorers was no more successful than Sunday school. The problem wasn't the name or design of the program, but the congregational culture in which it existed.[2] The failure of Bible Explorers forced us to examine the cultural realities concerning why people were no longer interested in spending several hours

---

2. I have found that drawing young people, particularly millennials, into church is a major concern for most congregations, so many of the examples I'm using will focus in this area.

at church on Sunday morning or enrolling their children in a weekly Bible program. We also discovered that parents were not interested in arguing with their children about going to Sunday school. Families were already overcommitted with school, sports, scouts, dance, and other activities. They viewed church participation as another item on the list, and when push came to shove, it was the item that got eliminated.

Another common place where we see congregations choosing the self-medicating path forward is in the changing of worship styles. How many congregations have shifted away from traditional worship to a more contemporary style in the hope of attracting more young people, only to discover that changing the style of worship alone doesn't work in achieving their goals? I remember when I was serving in my first call, back in the 1990s, the popular push was toward a worship style that was less liturgical and more rock concert. When we made changes to our worship life to fit in to what we perceived to be the popular desire, we found that our worship attendance numbers and visitor traffic didn't increase. It turned out that because nonliturgical worship was not indigenous to our congregation and none of our leaders (including me as the pastor) had any experience with it, we didn't do it well. When we returned to a liturgical style that included better execution of music and more engaging preaching, we grew. The issue wasn't the style of worship as much as the culture of worship that was indigenous to our congregation and greater context.

Or consider how many congregations have transformed their confirmation program from an every-week system to a once-a-month format only to discover that the number of students attending continues to decline. We have restructured our confirmation ministry several times in the past decade to address this problem, and nothing has seemed to work. We have gone from weekly to semimonthly to occasional retreats as a way of drawing more young people into confirmation, while the numbers continue to drop. The problems we are facing in the church are not that we're operating the wrong programs; it's that we are largely unaware of the contributing cultural factors that are holding us back from becoming vitalized and healthy. Loads of books have been written about the end of Christendom and movement into the postmodern era. We are all aware of the contextual transformations that have occurred. However, we have continued to operate out of a mindset that we simply need to find a new normal for being church, new programs or ministries that will finally appeal to people, new worship styles or structures that will lead to growth. But such pursuits continually fail us and leave us pastors fatigued and frustrated.

Let's be real: The church doesn't need to be fixed. The church doesn't need better programs. The church doesn't need to find ways to connect with or attract people. The church is called to stand as witness to the resurrection of Christ amid its cultural context, living as an alternative community drawing all people into full communion with God, others, and creation. Once the church identifies its mission and calling amid the cultural realities, then it becomes positioned to begin to create ways of life that point to and participate in God's salvific activity in the world today.

Much of what is contained in this book is not new information but an integration of interdisciplinary ideas, theories, systems, and practices necessary for generating vitalized congregations. My hope is that this information will become fodder for ongoing conversation between congregational and judicatory leaders and will lead to greater experimentation in working toward congregational vitality. In the ELCA, we have created a new model for redeveloping congregations called anchor church, in which vitalized congregations accompany struggling congregations toward cultural transformation. This book is intended to be a tool for the anchor church movement and for anyone working in cultural architecture or organizational development. God bless anyone who is engaging in the very difficult and challenging work of congregational development in the twenty-first century. May our efforts bear the fruit of love and life for all.

What You Can Expect from This Book

In chapter 1 we will explore the dis-ease of the current North American culture and its effects on human development. This exploration will lead us into a conversation with the fields of psychology and theology as they address healthy human development and call for a cultural awakening. As such, we will discuss a move from the head to the heart through the role of contemplative practices exercised within a congregational context.

In chapter 2 I will share a bit about the story of Abiding Hope, the congregation where I have served for the past sixteen years. My hope is that sharing a bit of our story will connect with your story so that as you read further, you can begin to apply the material in the book to your context. I will also share stories about our work in congregational vitality through accompanying three other congregations toward cultural transformation. I believe their struggles to be indicative of what many congregational leaders are facing these days.

Chapter 3 will begin to lead us through the practical aspects necessary for generating a congregational culture of vitality. We first create clarity regarding identity and purpose grounded in the *missio Dei* (mission of God). I will then walk you through a process for generating strong and compelling guiding statements on which the congregational culture will be constructed.

Chapter 4 begins our conversation regarding the concept of organizational intelligence as it relates to strategic cultural development. We will explore the wisdom of Russ Crabtree and Ron Heifetz as they relate to creating strategic plans to guide a congregation through cultural transformation.

In chapter 5 I will describe the anchor church initiative that we began at Abiding Hope and that has generated a movement within the ELCA in which healthy, vitalized congregations accompany struggling congregations in the journey toward vitality.

Chapter 6 is an exploration into other anchor church models for generating congregational vitality.

In the epilogue I share with you my hopes and dreams for the greater church and offer resources to aid you in your journey. The appendices are examples of resources that we'd like to make available to you as partners in Christ.

The Bias of the Book

You will undoubtedly discern as you read this book that I am a person of perpetual privilege. I am a large, vociferous, middle-aged, middle-class, white, educated, male living in an overwhelmingly white suburban context serving an overwhelmingly white, upper-middle class congregation in an overwhelmingly white Christian denomination. That is my context. I must confess that I am inexperienced in developing congregations that serve other contexts, such as multi-cultural, rural, inner-city/urban. Most of the sources and references utilized within this book relate to my particular context and experience.

I would be grateful to form relationships with brothers and sisters who have used the same or similar systems and principles outlined within this book to generate healthy and vitalized congregations in contexts different from my own. I encourage many books to be written, especially by persons of color, in the area of congregational vitality. I know that there is still much for me, and for all of us, to learn.

May the Spirit guide your reading of this book so that it might be a blessing to you and your ministry as God shapes you to be the cultural architect you are called to be.

I

EXPERIENCE REAL LIFE

Begin with the end in mind.

—Stephen Covey, *The 7 Habits of Highly Effective People*

I can't count the number of leadership books I've read or workshops I attended back in the 1990s and early 2000s. I can tell you that most of those books and workshops were of a secular or business nature, while very few were faith based. At that time, Stephen Covey's name became synonymous with leadership techniques and organizational development as he created *The 7 Habits of Highly Effective People*. The first of his habits was to be proactive, don't wait for problems to happen, be forward thinking to stay ahead of the problems. This is something we can all benefit from, no matter where we are in our ministries.

The second habit was the quotation above, "Begin with the end in mind."

This habit has always resounded with me. I have a difficult time diving into details until I know what outcome we seek to attain. Over the years, I have become increasingly frustrated because it seems many within the church don't know what we're trying to achieve. It seems that the focus is often on getting more people into church or paying the bills or doing a service project (such as buying mosquito nets for Africa or addressing global climate change) because it's easier to rally around such things.

While I am in favor of growing the church, paying bills, and serving others, we first need to generate clarity for why the church even exists before we dive into action. What is the call and role of the church? I think it's safe to say that the old role of the church was to save people from hell. But when was the last time someone joined your church because they were afraid of going to hell? I don't see that as a significant impetus these days for drawing people to church, at least not in the mainline traditions. And if our purpose is simply to do good deeds in the community and the world, why do people need the church to do that? A significant part of our problem is that we don't know how to make a case (or even what case to make) for being a part of the Jesus community in the twenty-first century.

If you were to knock on doors and invite people to church, what reason would you give them? We welcome everyone, no exceptions. We have good music and preaching. We have a vibrant youth program. Really? That's it. Would such things make you or your kids want to be part of the church? Where is the vision for something different, something that generates life, something that transforms individuals and ultimately the world? That's the language we need, but it has to be built out of a clear vision for what such a community might be.

As I articulated in the introduction, God's goal for humanity and for the cosmos is life, abundant life, as Jesus tells us in John 10:10. I don't believe that Jesus was simply talking about after we die. I believe that Jesus was talking about right here, right now. We have been conditioned to read Scripture through the lens of doctrine created during and following the fourth and fifth centuries CE. Those doctrines have generated a faith tradition focused primarily on the sins and salvation of the individual. I believe that we need to set some of this doctrinal stuff aside (remember that I wrote above that we need radical death and resurrection) so that we can read the Scripture through a communal, cultural lens. When we do this, we discover that Jesus was concerned with creating a community of people who choose to live differently from the dominant culture as a means of transforming all lives in love. By individualizing faith through doctrinal decree, the church turned Christianity into an exclusive system of reward and punishment that reaches beyond death. This fear-based system was certainly a convenient and effective method for controlling the largely uneducated populace, but since the rise of the baby boomers and subsequent generations who are more highly educated than previous generations, that old, fear-based system no longer holds water.

In my experience, people are less concerned about circumstances after they die and more concerned about the matters of today. The people I encounter may ponder here or there about what happens after they die, but realistically they are more concerned about their lives, their kids' lives, their grandkids' lives *right now*. Many feel that even though they have achieved the American dream and enjoy success, something is still missing. People feel out of alignment. Here in Littleton, Colorado, we have a problem. We live in the community of Columbine High School, Platte Canyon High School, Deer Creek Middle

School, Arapahoe High School, and the STEM School of Highlands Ranch. Each of these schools has experienced a mass shooting, and members of Abiding Hope, the congregation I serve, were present at each of them. A good friend of mine, a psychotherapist in our community who works exclusively with teen boys, tells me that I'd be horrified to know how many school catastrophes have been averted because of the intervention of schools, the sheriff's department, and therapists. Our local law enforcement deals with the threat of copycat violence on a regular basis.

In addition to mass violence, Colorado ranks among the top ten states in suicide annually.[1] I frequently tell people that a week does not go by that our congregation's staff does not deal with suicide in some form. Even as I write this, I just learned two days ago of a fourteen-year-old member of our congregation who tried to hang herself. Trust me, dealing with suicide never gets easier. On the contrary, I grieve deeply each and every time I learn of someone threatening, attempting, or completing suicide. A few years ago, I received a phone call from the woman who leads our survivors of suicide support group. She told me that three new people had arrived at one of the group sessions. After telling me their names, we began to discuss their cases. Regarding one woman, I said, "Oh, she found her husband hanged in the garage," to which the counselor corrected me, saying, "No, her husband shot himself in front of her." I immediately began to weep because I realized that we had so many suicides in our congregation and community that I was beginning to confuse them.

Every time I preach, I am aware that someone at the worship service may be contemplating suicide. I am very careful with my words and always seek to convey a message of hope. We

1. "Suicides in Colorado: 2017 Trends," Colorado Health Institute, September 12, 2018, https://tinyurl.com/yxvdzwzp.

speak openly at Abiding Hope about the issue of suicide and provide countless resources to individuals and families for both prevention and remediation. We work with schools, therapists, and other organizations in our community to address this ongoing problem. It grieves me deeply that I serve as a pastor in a community where so many people choose to give up on life. Often when I share my personal anguish over this reality, people will try to comfort me by saying something like, "You are doing everything you can," or, "It's not your fault." I get angry when I hear such comments. Even though I know the person is attempting to help me, my pain is a result of the love and passion for human beings that God has poured into me. If one person gives up on life, then all of us should grieve. I believe the church is called not only to be a beacon of light amid the darkness, but to be a change agent for the greater culture so that all may live full and whole lives as children of God. Until that vision is realized, the church has much work to do!

What Are People Seeking?

While the people of our community might be seeking something, most cannot articulate the something they seek. There appears to be an emptiness, a void in people's lives, even though they may self-report that they are content with their family, job, and finances. My predecessor and mentor, Rick Barger, tells the story of engaging first-time attendees following a worship service and asking them what brought them to church. Their response was to say that they were sensing that "something was missing" and were seeking a connection to a "spiritual community" that would be "the icing on the cake" for their otherwise wonderful lives.[2] Rick correctly points out that these people

2. Rick Barger, *A New and Right Spirit: Creating an Authentic Church in a Consumer Culture* (Lanham, MD: Rowman & Littlefield, 2005), 46.

were approaching the church as consumers, viewing it as a commodity to be used to attain personal happiness. Therein lies the problem.

As a society, we try to fill ourselves up from the outside only to discover perpetual emptiness. Futile attempt after futile attempt at attaining fullness finally results in a learned helplessness that generates feelings of despair, anxiety, or depression. This causes the individual to feel as though they are a failure, or that their life is not worth living, or even that society as a whole is no good. I certainly see this in my own congregation. Furthermore, the rising rates of depression and anxiety among the general population support the occurrence of this phenomenon. A quick scan of the data on websites such as the National Institute of Mental Health (www.nimh.nih.gov) or the Anxiety and Depression Association of America (www.adaa.org) reveals disturbing statistics regarding the psycho-emotional state of the American population. Even more disturbing is the increase of anxiety and depression among teens and young adults. The American Psychological Association reports, "Ninety-five percent of college counseling center directors surveyed said the number of students with significant psychological problems is a growing concern in their center or on campus, according to the latest Association for University and College Counseling Center Directors survey of counseling center directors."[3] Our individualized and consumeristic culture is killing us, literally! We desperately need a cultural transformation, but how can this happen, and who is called to lead such a transformation?

While much conversation has occurred over recent decades regarding the dangers of the current individualistic and consumeristic culture, most people are largely unaware that they continually and repetitively turn to other individualized and

---

3. "College Students' Mental Health Is a Growing Concern, Study Finds," *Monitor on Psychology* 44 (June 2013), https://tinyurl.com/r4lw2x8.

consumeristic methods in an attempt to free themselves from the deadly ills of the culture. As someone who has been traveling to Haiti for over fifteen years and was present during the 2010 earthquake, I'm familiar with the many challenges facing the Haitian people. As such, I see a parallel with the current cultural realities in the United States and the 2010 cholera outbreak in the Haitian rural communities. The largely uneducated Haitian community didn't understand that the source of their illness was the cholera bacteria in the water. When people became infected with the disease, they began to dehydrate, and so they naively drank more of the infected water, ultimately resulting in death.

The same dynamic appears to be happening in our affluent American context. The individualized, consumer-driven culture has infected people, leaving them without a sense of identity or purpose. To discover themselves, they turn to more individualized and consumer-driven products (even within the church!), ultimately resulting in emotional and spiritual death. Just as the Haitian people did not understand that the cause of the disease was in the water—they just knew that they were sick and thirsty—our people don't seem to realize that the cause of the disease is in their selfish pursuits; they just know that they are empty and afraid and don't want to feel sick any more.

In dealing with the cholera epidemic, the solution lay in educating people about the cause of the disease (bacteria in the water), drawing them into new practices that would prevent the disease (boiling or treating water, washing hands), and treating the infected person effectively when it did occur (use of antibiotics and hydration with clean water). Similarly, we as the church bear the responsibility of being the prophetic voice that points to the ills of our current ways of life while casting a vision for what it looks like to be the new humanity, God's people within our world today. We also must provide the structures and systems that will support people as they move into the new way of life so that they can withstand the hurricane force gales of the current, deadly culture that threatens to infect us all.

I believe there is a direct correlation between the breakdown of the church over the past half-century and the increase of cultural toxicity. What is the medium within society through which people can explore the depths of their identity and purpose? Where do we turn to explore the meaning of life? How do we garner the resources to address the reality of suffering and pain within ourselves and our context? We've seen some people turn to various forms of addiction to find meaning or to mask the pain. The church itself throughout history has not been immune from supporting and carrying purposes that were imperfect; it has participated in the great evils of racism, sexism, and classism, resulting in indescribable division, violence, and destruction.

The church generally has sought to provide common values around which culture and community could be built. However, there don't appear to be any common or shared values today to serve as guideposts for what it means to be human. We are failing to heed the warnings of our deteriorating culture, demonstrated through heightened political divisions, a rise in racial and religious tensions, mass shootings, teen suicides, and a generalized feeling of dis-ease. Instead, we choose to treat these symptoms as though they can be expunged through therapeutic methods so that as a result society will become "normal." It's not working!

Why Do I Matter?

A well-known cartoon in the *New Yorker* magazine depicts a dog sitting attentively before a guru in the lotus position in front of a cave at the top of a mountain. The guru responds to the dog, saying, "The bone is not the reward—digging for the bone is the reward."[4]

Throughout human history, people have sought to ascertain the meaning of life. Another form of the question of meaning is to ask, Why do I matter? The Latin root for *matter* is *mater*, which means "source, origin, mother." The quest for meaning is actually a pursuit to find our source, to understand and appreciate the origin of humanity, and to truly discover ourselves and what we're here to be and to do. In his seminal book, *Man's Search for Meaning*, which he composed following his release from Nazi concentration camps, Viktor Frankl writes:

> A thought transfixed me: for the first time in my life I saw the truth as it is set into song by so many poets, proclaimed as the final wisdom by so many thinkers. The truth—that love is the ultimate and the highest goal to which man can aspire. Then I grasped the meaning of the greatest secret that human poetry and human thought and belief have to impart: *The salvation of man is through love and in love.*[5]

Despite our best attempts through psychotherapy or self-reflection, the human self is not something that can be discovered inwardly through introspection but only outside oneself through *ekstasis*, through communion with God and other. In other words, the human self is encountered and discovered through love.

Frankl explains it best when he goes on to write,

> I wish to stress that the true meaning of life is to be discovered in the world rather than within man or his own psyche, as though it were a closed system. I have termed this constitutive characteristic

4. Michael Maslin, *The New Yorker*, June 23, 2014.
5. Viktor E. Frankl, *Man's Search for Meaning* (Boston: Beacon, 2006), 37.

"the self-transcendence of human existence." It denotes the fact that being human always points, and is directed, to something, or someone, other than oneself—be it a meaning to fulfill or another human being to encounter. The more one forgets himself—by giving himself to a cause to serve or another person to love—the more human he is and the more he actualizes himself.[6]

Life, Liberty, and the Pursuit of Happiness

Unfortunately, dedicating oneself to a life of love reified through authentic worship, intentional relationships, acts of service, and radical generosity has been far from the normal way of living in our current society. American culture has equated a meaningful life with becoming happy through the pursuit of rampant individualism and consumerism, focused on chasing self-gratification, striving to accumulate for oneself, and seeking to discover oneself through introspection and self-reflection. What I mean is, I don't think we discover our true selves on our own but through interaction, contemplation, and engagement with God, others, and creation. Empty individualistic pursuits have resulted in large-scale emotional disturbance, substance abuse, and various acts of violence throughout the American landscape.

For more than a century, the increasing pollution of the American culture has been inadvertently reinforced by the field of psychology primarily dedicating itself to identifying and eradicating pathologies within the human psyche believed to inhibit one's pursuit of happiness. Such motivation has primarily been driven by the thinking of Sigmund Freud, who held "that mental health is just the absence of mental illness," as Martin Seligman puts it. Freud was a follower of philosopher Arthur Schopenhauer (1788–1860). Both believed that happiness was an

6. Frankl, *Man's Search for Meaning*, 110–11.

illusion and that the best we could ever hope for was to keep our misery and suffering to a minimum. Let there be no doubt about this: traditional psychotherapy is not designed to produce well-being; it is designed just to curtail misery, which is itself no small task.[7] I'm not suggesting that psychotherapy should not be used when necessary. I'm simply stating that our reliance on psychotherapy to mitigate our problems in pursuit of happiness will not transform the toxicity of our culture, which, I believe, to be at the root of our problems. This is akin to a quotation often attributed to Desmond Tutu: "There comes a point when we need to stop just pulling people out of the river. We need to go up the river and find out why they keep falling in."

From Curing Pathology to Generating Well-Being

University of Pennsylvania psychologist Martin Seligman entered the field of psychology with the same intent as most:

> I have spent most of my life working on psychology's venerable goal of relieving misery and uprooting the disabling conditions of life. Truth be told, this can be a drag. Taking the psychology of misery to heart—as you must when you work on depression, alcoholism, schizophrenia, trauma, and the panoply of suffering that makes up psychology-as-usual's primary material—can be a vexation to the soul. While we do more than our bit to increase the well-being of our clients, psychology-as-usual typically does not do much for the well-being of the practitioners. If anything changes in the practitioner, it is a personality shift toward depression.[8]

---

7. Martin E. P. Seligman, *Flourish: A Visionary New Understanding of Happiness and Well-Being* (New York: Simon & Schuster, 2011), 183.
8. Seligman, *Flourish*, 1.

Seligman professes that he set out early in his career conducting psychological laboratory experimentation that lacked application in a manner that would significantly benefit humanity. Dissatisfied with the notion that alleviating symptoms was the best that the school of psychology had to offer humanity, Seligman refocused his work on discovering the source, the root cause for human happiness. What do those who are happy possess, and can the qualities of happiness be taught or conveyed in others? What would happen if we moved from trying to correct what is wrong in people to motivating them toward positive traits that produce fulfillment and happiness? Seligman claims to have had a breakthrough during a conversation with his five-year old daughter, Nikki.

> I realized that raising Nikki was not about correcting her short-comings. She could do that herself. Rather, my purpose in raising her was to nurture this precocious strength she had displayed—I call it seeing into the soul, but the jargon is social intelligence—and help her to mold her life around it. Such a strength, fully grown, would be a buffer against her weaknesses and against the storms of life that would inevitably come her way. Raising children, I knew now, was far more than just fixing what was wrong with them. It was about identifying and amplifying their strengths and virtues, and helping them find the niche where they can live these positive traits to the fullest. . . . Can parents and teachers use this science that makes life worth living? Can parents and teachers use this science to raise strong, resilient children ready to take their place in a world in which more opportunities for fulfillment are available? Can adults teach themselves better ways to happiness and fulfillment?"[9]

9. Martin E. P. Seligman, *Authentic Happiness: Using the New Positive Psychology to Realize Your Potential for Lasting Fulfillment* (New York: Simon & Schuster, 2002), 28–29.

Please don't misunderstand. I'm not advocating that the church be an organization to help persons become "happy." That's actually been part of our ongoing problem, as we've created programs to cater to the consumeristic desires of individuals. To the contrary, the work of Seligman in positive psychology gives valuable, empirical data supporting the biblical notion that human beings, who created *imago Dei* (in the image of God) exist to live lives dedicated beyond the self, toward intimate relationships and sacrificial service. I am asserting that it is not an accident that science now proves that human beings who have deep relationships, who participate in meaningful endeavors larger than self, and who use their gifts in service of others have generally greater well-being than those who don't. I believe this occurs because relationships, service, and generosity are the created purpose for every human life. The church has missed the mark by focusing on eradicating the "sins" of people instead of generating a culture that maximizes the gifts and strengths of people, and then unleashing those gifts into the greater community.

Experience Real Life

If, as Reggie McNeal alerted us, life is the aim, the goal, the desired outcome, we must ask: What does real life look like, and how do we attain it? More precisely, what is the church's role in accompanying people in the journey to experience real life? While it's important that we as the church stay grounded in Scripture and theology, there is a deep resonance between what Scripture describes as the purpose of human life and what the social sciences have discovered. Research and writing by social scientists such as Seligman provide the empirical data demonstrating that those who are in deeper relationships (thus allowing themselves to be vulnerable), participate in groups and projects larger than themselves, and engage in acts of service and generosity tend to have a greater sense of wellness and a more positive regard toward life than those who don't have such experiences. This positive regard does not eliminate suffering but introduces joy, hope, peace, and contentment amid life's struggles and difficulties. Isn't it interesting that such ecstatic principles of love, service, and generosity are contained throughout Scripture? For examples, see 1 John 15:13; Matthew 22:37–39; Romans 12; 1 Corinthians 13; Colossians 3:12–17. In fact, when we examine the life of Jesus, we see these very principles lived out in all that he did and called his followers to do, ultimately culminating in the cross.

During the dissertation project that I conducted in pursuit of a doctor of ministry degree, I learned that simply serving or being generous is not enough to result in long-term personal transformation. I asked twenty subjects to orient themselves toward one other person in a posture of service and generosity for a period of six weeks. Through narrative inquiry, I measured the changes experienced by the servants. During the six-week period, seventeen of the participants chose to participate in weekly discussion groups regarding their service, while three chose not to participate in the groups but still engaged in serving. All who participated in small group conversations self-reported significant personal transformation (e.g., greater hope, sense of purpose, became more loving), while the three who did not participate in group conversations self-reported no change. This demonstrated that service and generosity in isolation do not lead to lasting transformation.

Service and generosity must be coupled with some form of processing one's experiences for lasting transformation to occur. Such processing can take place in groups, in one-on-one conversations, or even through journaling. In addition to calling people to serve and to be generous, we must create opportunities for reflection and processing regarding their experiences, because this makes one aware of the value of service and generosity to self. Recognizing that doing for others isn't enough, nor is introspection on its own, Richard Rohr adeptly calls his organization Center for Action *and* Contemplation. We are called to act in love toward God, others, and creation, and then contemplate those experiences.

One woman in my research project chose to serve a friend dying from an autoimmune disorder by helping her to plan her funeral. The friend's husband found the task too painful to do, so the participant chose to help her friend with this deeply personal and painful task. To make it "less weird," they also worked together to plan the participant's funeral. The participant said, "I'm going to die someday too, and it just seemed natural that we would do this loving thing for one another." This demonstrated that the participant did not see serving her friend as one-directional but as a mutual walking together. Also, the participant reported that she always left her time with her friend feeling as though she had received far more than she gave. The participant, an introvert, said that during this time she also had a lot of houseguests, which caused her great stress. Serving her friend helped her to cope with her stress of dealing with her houseguests and assisted her to keep things in perspective.

Another woman who had been married for thirty years decided to serve her husband as their relationship was going through transition. While serving him, she made it a daily discipline to read Scripture passages about serving. She realized that while she had been a servant throughout her life, she tended to minimize herself in serving others. She recognized in Scripture that serving others was never intended to be a minimizing of self. She then felt more empowered and confident in her relationship with her husband, that her role was not simply to do things for him but to be proactive in helping him in his own growth and formation as a person. This new perception gave her a greater love and appreciation for herself, as well as newfound confidence and strength.

We know that the real life we seek to generate for human beings within a congregational context is not about consumption (participation in programs for personal advancement or gain) or even happiness (experiencing more pleasure than pain). The real life we seek through participation in a congregation is a deeper awareness and/or experience of oneness with God, one another, and creation, deriving from *and* resulting in orienting one's gifts, resources, and abilities in love and service toward God, one another, and creation. Such self-emptying, often called *kenosis*, is modeled within the Trinitarian relationship, in which Father, Son, and Holy Spirit each continually pours self into the other. This uninhibited flow of love from the Divine is extended into humanity with the expectation that human beings participate in emptying self into others. The irony is that kenotic behavior, or self-emptying, produces a sense of fullness, whereas blocking the flow of love through self-focused neediness and consumption creates emptiness. Because humanity was created in the image of God (*imago Dei*), we must act and behave in the same manner as God to be whole or well.

In her discussion of the mysticism of St. Bonaventure, Elaine Heath writes,

> Creation is the joyous overflow of the relationship of Father, Son, and Holy Spirit, as water bubbles forth from a fountain. Originating as an idea of the Father, each created thing mirrors some aspect of Christ, and through the Holy Spirit returns to God in consummation as it fulfills its intended creaturely purpose. . . . To put it in contemporary terms, when creatures and ecosystems function

in healthy interdependence, the dynamic life of God is revealed. When creatures and ecosystems are hindered or oppressed, that life is obscured.

I believe it's safe to say that what we've been experiencing throughout society in recent decades is obscured life. Heath continues,

> Humanity is both clay and divine breath, made of a composite of body and soul, so that not only does humanity contain within itself all "lower" forms of creation, but in Christ humanity also becomes mediator for the return of all things to the Creator. Humanity bears a unique responsibility to facilitate the healing of creation. . . . Laying the foundation of an interdependent, redemptive relationship between humans and the rest of creation, Bonaventure's vision of salvation flows from Christ through the Church, out into the world.[10]

If we understand salvation (deriving from the Greek word *sōtēria* or *sōzō*) as "being made whole, well, complete" versus the notion of "being saved" (which often connotes going to heaven when we die), our ecclesiology shifts from saving people from hell to participating in God's restorative mission of drawing all things into oneness. Such a perspective necessarily debunks the notion that one can be whole individually or in isolation. Think of someone you love deeply. Could you be whole without them? Of course not. In fact, being with them, loving them, serving them is a key part of what *makes* you whole. This is the basis of *ekstasis* (from which we get the word *ecstasy*), which means to "stand outside" self. When our general life orientation is focused inward, on satisfying our own wants or desires, we cannot attain wholeness. We are whole through active emptying of

10. Elaine Heath, *The Mystic Way of Evangelism: A Contemplative Vision for Christian Outreach*, 2nd ed. (Grand Rapids: Baker Academic, 2017), 93–96.

self (kenosis) into God, other, and creation. This is the path to salvation.

Now, I am not saying that we produce salvation for ourselves. Our wholeness is a gift from God, generated by God, delivered by God, but we get to live and actively participate within it. This is what St. Paul meant when he wrote in Philippians 2:12, "Work out your own salvation." He's not saying that we generate salvation within ourselves, any more than I am generating my body when I engage in a physical workout. He's calling us to participate actively in our salvation (our oneness with God and all things), to put it to use in generating new life. I am sometimes concerned that we Lutherans place so much emphasis on salvation being all about God's activity that we overlook our called role as children of God to participate within God's restorative salvation of the cosmos. Yes, God's love for us, our very lives, and our oneness with God and all things come as a gift. But we are called to use that gift as we partner with God in the restoration of oneness with all the creation.

Throughout my twenty-five years of ordained ministry, I have not done a great job in leading people toward *ekstasis*. Most of my ministry has been focused on the head more than the heart, more on comprehension of beliefs than dwelling in oneness with God. I have sought to teach and explain doctrine and theology more than invite people into God experiences. In fact, over the years, I have been largely dismissive of *ekstasis*, understanding it to be an individualized, emotional experience that serves no greater good than to give an individual a misguided, even delusional, confirmation that they are connected to God. Boy, was I naive and ignorant.

Heath has helped me to gain a deeper and more authentic understanding of these concepts.

Christian mysticism is grounded in the church, the body of Christ. It is the God-initiated experience of being moved beyond oneself into greater depths of divine love. This movement results in an inward transformation of wholeness and integration and outward life of holiness, an increasing love of God and neighbor.[11]

You can see from this explanation that an ecstatic, mystical experience is not at all about the individual in isolation, but about God's very essence being experienced by an individual as an expression of deep love or deep belonging, resulting in outward movement toward oneness with all, which is the *missio Dei* (mission of God).

As a child, I remember feeling a deep connection with God, others, and creation. I felt that I could hear God speak to me at night when I was in bed or in moments when I would pray alone. This connection to God led me to talk openly to plants and animals, appreciating their beauty as I viewed them as an extension of myself. I was deeply wounded by movies such as *Bambi* or *Dumbo* (Why do the parents always seem to die in Disney movies?), as I felt a deep connection to family and friends and could empathize deeply with the grief and pain of others. I even believed that the weather was somehow connected to my own thoughts and feelings. But when I spoke openly to others about such things, I quickly learned that this way of thinking was not accepted and often regarded as being weird or even crazy. I learned that I would be rewarded by teachers, pastors, parents, and peers more for my cognitive and intellectual abilities than for what I would now call my spiritual awareness. To be honest, I became a pastor because I was intrigued by theology, but as I now reflect back, there was a yearning deep within me to reconnect with the spiritual awareness of my childhood. I thank God that in recent years I have been blessed by the work

11. Heath, *Mystic Way of Evangelism*, 6.

of persons such as Richard Rohr, Elaine Heath, Rob Bell, and others who have given me permission to move from my head to my heart.

Trust, Not Belief; Experience, Not Understanding

Through my own personal journey into the contemplative life, I began to feel challenged to find new ways of incorporating contemplation into the congregational experience. I now believe that the contemplative life will be the future of the Christian movement by providing opportunities for people to discern God's presence and to be called into actionable love toward God, neighbor, and creation. Such a pursuit is far more organic than creating programs and inviting people into them. It will require that we spend long amounts of time training people in the art of contemplation so that they are perceiving God at all times and in all circumstances. "Church activity" will not take place in a building or facility but in the everyday activities at home, work, school, neighborhood, and beyond. In this regard, the church serves as the vessel in aiding people to journey paths of self-discovery as experienced through worship, relationships, service, and generosity.

I could be wrong, but, in my experience, the church has placed great emphasis on right teaching (orthodoxy) as the path toward salvation. To be saved from hell, people need to believe the "right things" about God and about themselves as sinners. Such an approach has resulted in Scripture, theology, and faith becoming objects to be studied, understood, and ultimately enacted. This led to the notion that before you can "act" as a Christian (orthopraxy), you must first understand and believe as a Christian (orthodoxy). That's why we put so much weight on educating our children through Sunday school and confirmation. Before they could become active members of the congregation, they had to be properly indoctrinated. This idea is built out of the premise that thinking precedes essence. Instead of clergy being guides or doulas leading people in and through God experiences, clergy became the resident Bible scholars and theologians responsible for ensuring that parishioners be educated within orthodoxy.

To cement such an emphasis, the church openly and actively proclaimed that those who do not believe and hence do not act properly would ultimately be condemned to hell for all eternity. This way of thinking worked to control many within the populace, until recent educated generations began to actively reject fear-driven ideas regarding God. Today, many millennials want nothing to do with fear-driven theology because it doesn't make rational sense that a God of love would condemn most of humanity for not believing or acting properly.

My most memorable encounter with this sort of pushback came from a very bright autistic confirmand (he's now in his mid-twenties) whose mother made him come talk to the pastor because he was telling his parents that he did not want to continue in our confirmation ministry or be confirmed because "There is no God." I asked the young man, "Why don't you believe in God?" He replied, "You believe that God is about love, right?" I said, "Of course," thinking to myself, "OK, we're on the right path." He then said, "But the church teaches that God sends people to hell, right?" Thinking to myself, "Uh oh," I replied, "Yes, the church has taught that." His following comment hit me between the eyes. "You want me to believe that God is love, created me out of love, and continues to love me, but if I do not believe in God the right way then your God of love will send me to hell for all eternity. Am I getting this right?"

I knew immediately that I was outmatched. This thirteen-year-old autistic kid had just dismantled Christian doctrine and dogma with simple reasoning. Wouldn't a God of love do what-ever it takes to create, preserve, and sustain life? Why would a God of love give up on someone simply because of their belief system? Would you give up on someone you loved, deeply loved, purely because of what they believed? Wouldn't you choose to remain in relationship and continue to love them? I asked the young man, "Do you believe in the power of love?" He said, "Yes." I said, "Then let's not use the word *God*. Let's just say that you believe in love and love is your God. Can you do that?" This very bright, youthful teacher of mine smiled and said, "Yes. I can do that." He was confirmed the next May.

Instead of seeking to *indoctrinate* people, what if we *encultur-ate* people into a way of life that produces life? The concept of indoctrination is based on creating orthodoxy, or right beliefs, through proper teaching that will result in orthopraxy, or right living. Why does belief necessarily precede doing? Doesn't doing or being precede thinking? Don't we live first and then reflect on our living and its impact on our lives? Furthermore, where does the heart come into play? Are we simply minds that think and bodies that do? Certainly, the human experience involves more than just thoughts and actions. What is the value of emotions, passions, drive, yearnings? Unfortunately, the church has vilified such heart matters, even calling desire the root of sin (read about Augustine's doctrine of original sin and the concept of concupiscence). Was Jesus driven more by head, heart, or doing? That's an unfair question, because we can see the integration of all three centers within the life of Jesus. The move from indoctrination to enculturation places experience before thinking or believing.

Enculturation is the process of immersing people into a way of life while aiding them in becoming fully aware of self, God, and others as they experience life. Instead of placing the focus on belief, attention is drawn to experiences as they relate to God, others, and creation. This experiential approach is necessarily relational, as no person exists in isolation, and the path toward self-discovery lies in relationships beyond ourselves.

God's self-identification implies that God cannot be understood, only experienced through relationship ("I am the God of your ancestors, the God of Abraham, Isaac, and Jacob," Exod 3:6). Thinking does not precede essence or existence. Essence, existence, and experience precede thinking. We experience life long before we are able to reflect on or contemplate life. Jesus didn't explain God or theology or even human existence to his followers and then tell them to go live it. He didn't create doctrine or dogma and then hold class sessions every day. He simply started by saying, "Come and see," or, "Come, follow me," and then led his followers into experiences, on which they then contemplated and reflected. As his followers experienced the healings, feeding of multitudes, and casting out of demons, he told them stories or parables about human existence to help them begin to perceive and contemplate the God activity within both the stories and their own experiences. The parables of the good Samaritan (Luke 10:25–37), the prodigal son (Luke 15:11–32), and the workers in the vineyard (Matt 20:1–16) all demonstrate the heart of God to serve, to forgive, and to include vis-à-vis the world's divisive and destructive hierarchical systems that incorporate some while ostracizing others. By enculturating the disciples into a new way of life as an alternative to the contemporary world culture, Jesus was laying the foundation for systematically transforming the greater culture, not through information but through personal re-creation.

Furthermore, I believe that Jesus didn't tell people to believe but to trust (the Greek verb *pisteuō* can be translated as "believe," "have faith," or "trust"). The notion of believing largely connotes a cognitive exercise that does not necessarily affect a person's life. Do you believe in ghosts? Do you believe in life on other planets? Do you believe in God? These questions are perceived to be inquiring about what one thinks rather than how one chooses to orient one's life. If I suddenly believe that life exists on other planets, I'm not going to do anything different today than I did yesterday.

Trust, however, is a different thing all together. First of all, trust implies a relationship between a trustor and a trustee. Trust is also built out of experience between the two parties. One is trusted because one has demonstrated that one is trustworthy. When trust is broken due to lies or deception, it becomes increasingly difficult for the trustor to remain in the trusting relationship. In fact, trust is one of the foundational aspects to all relationships. Trusting God will necessarily affect how I live my life because I trust God to forgive me, I trust God to guide me in my life, and I trust God to ensure that love and life win. Within such a trusting relationship, I will be a different person than if such a trust in God did not exist.

To mine deeper into this concept of trust versus belief, let's explore the passage that most Christians think of when regarding the notion of believing, John 3:14–21. The very first Bible verse I memorized as a child was John 3:16. I learned it from the old King James Version, which said, "For God so loved the world, that he gave his only begotten Son, that whosoever believeth in him should not perish, but have everlasting life." I remember during my youth seeing the guy with the multicolored wig holding up the John 3:16 sign at nationally televised football games, often in the stands behind the goalposts. In recent years, it's not uncommon for players to write "John 3:16" on the black tape under their eyes so that when the camera pans in closely on their faces, viewers can see this call to believe.

There's no question that those who encourage others to read John 3:16 are striving to help people to be saved from the fires of hell. But what if the Gospel of John, especially chapter 3, is not about "believing in" Jesus but instead "trusting God" and being drawn into Christ?

It's critically important in both translating and interpreting passages from John that we proceed with a clear understanding of John 1:1–18, commonly called the prologue, which begins, "In the beginning was the Logos [Word], and the Logos was toward the God, and the Logos was God" (my translation). The Logos (Word) stands as the idea in the mind of God for the creation of humanity, referenced in Genesis 1:3, "Let there be light." Since the sun, moon, and stars are created on day four, the light of day one must be interpreted by the author of the Fourth Gospel to be the Logos or idea in the mind of God that necessarily precedes the act of creating. The Fourth Gospel is a new-creation story. The prologue goes on to prove this point by saying in John 1:3–5, 9–14:

> All things through him happened, and without him nothing happened. What happened in him was life, and the life was the Light of all humanity. And the Light in the darkness shines, and the darkness cannot overcome it. . . . The true light, which enlightens all humanity, was coming into the *kosmos* [human culture]. In the *kosmos* [human culture] he was, and although the *kosmos* [human culture] through him happened, the *kosmos* [human culture] did not know him. Into his own he came, and his own did not receive him. But to those who did receive him, he gave the ability to become children of God, to those who trusted into his name, not out of blood or out of the will of the flesh or out of the will of man but out of God were born. And the Logos became flesh and tented in [among] us, and we have seen his glory, the glory as of a one-

of-a-kind offspring from a father, full of giftedness and truth. (my translation)

The author of the Fourth Gospel sets the entire book up to be a narrative about how God's idea for humanity (Logos) became enfleshed and entered human culture as the means to rebirth humanity according to the divine design from the beginning. Notice that the above translation of the Greek *kosmos* as "human culture" instead of "world." Historically in Greek, *kosmos* has referred to an ordered system. Pythagoras was the first to use the term to refer to the universe as he mathematically proved that the objects in the heavens were connected and affected one another within an ordered system. "World" is not recommended as the translation of *kosmos* in the Fourth Gospel, as the term *world* contemporarily connotes the physical earth. The author of the Fourth Gospel was using the term to represent the ordered human systems that have become corrupted by greed, hatred, fear, and violence, resulting in the death and destruction of that which God creates. The author of the Fourth Gospel is driving home the point that the Logos becomes enfleshed to rebirth a new humanity that will create just human systems conducive to life for all. That's why a more reasonable, relevant, and sound translation of *kosmos* is "human culture."

Also, when reading the Fourth Gospel, it's essential that we remember that in no way is the author depicting or representing some process by which flawed, sinful human beings must believe or act in the right way (orthodoxy or orthopraxy) to gain salvation, that is, going to heaven after we die. Quite the contrary, according to the Fourth Gospel, God views humanity as God's children who have missed the mark (Greek *hamartia*) by not living according to our true identity and purpose, which is to create a human culture conducive to life for all. The death of Jesus the Messiah on Good Friday is the end of the old moral order governed by hierarchy, violence, and division; Holy Saturday stands as a necessary gap between the old and the new; and the resurrection of Jesus on Sunday, the first day of the week or the eighth day, depicts the dawn of the new creation and the birth of the new humanity governed solely by love and inclusion of all. When we read the Fourth Gospel through this lens, each passage comes to life as we become drawn into a narrative of new creation, new birth, new life that fills us with hope, joy, peace, and love for all.

John 3 begins with Nicodemus, a Pharisee and member of the temple council, coming to see Jesus during the dark of night. The reference to darkness must not be missed here. The Light, the same Light referenced in Genesis 1 on the first day of creation and which Jesus came to bring to the world, has not yet been revealed or unleashed. Nicodemus is depicted not as a tempter or accuser, but rather he is sincere in his quest to discover who this Jesus is, as perhaps he too has been expectantly waiting for the "anointed one" of God who will inaugurate a new day for Israel. However, despite Nicodemus's education, position as a leader, and desire for a new day, he cannot understand what Jesus attempts to tell him in John 3:3, "Without being born anew/from above [*anōthen*], no one can see the reign of God" (my translation). This statement utterly confuses Nicodemus because he cannot get his brain around the idea of rebirth.

We know, based on the above commentary of John 1, that Jesus is talking about a new creation, a new birth for humanity derived entirely from the Logos, the idea, the vision in God's mind for humanity. However, Nicodemus remains stuck on the idea of being born from a woman. Jesus then begins to explain to Nicodemus what he means by first referencing baptism, "being born of water and Spirit," which will become the process by which new human beings are birthed. Regardless of Jesus's explanations, Nicodemus just can't get it.

Starting in verse 14, Jesus gets into the nitty-gritty:

> And just as Moses lifted up the serpent in the wilderness, so the Son of the Human Being will be lifted up, in order that all who are trusting [*pisteuōn*] have a life of the ages. So, for God loved [*ēgapēsen*] the human culture [*kosmon*], that the one-of-a-kind son was given, in order that all who are trusting [*pisteuōn*] into him not be obliterated but have a life of the ages. For God did not send the Son into the human culture in order to condemn the human culture, but in order that the human culture be made whole [*sōthē*, from *sōzō*] through him. (John 3:14–17, my translation)

Notice that in both verses 15 and 16 that *pisteuōn* is translated as "trusting" instead of "believing." The misinterpretation of the Fourth Gospel is tied to the doctrinal position that right belief leads to individual salvation, which has fueled a substitutionary atonement theory, meaning that if humans believe rightly in Jesus, then their filth and transgressions get imputed onto Jesus's punishment in the cross while Jesus's righteousness gets imputed onto them. That is, if a filthy, flawed human doesn't believe rightly, then that one perishes into the fires of hell for all eternity. Sadly, most, if not all, have been taught to interpret John 3:16 this way at some point.

Thus, for our purposes, "trust" is a far-preferred translation of *pisteuō*. To be clear, the hearer isn't being called to trust Jesus. The hearer is being called to trust *into* Jesus,[12] to trust God *like* or *as* Jesus trusted God. The recipient of our trust is God: the orig-

---

12. I think that the author uses the Greek term *eis* to imply movement as opposed to a static position. Through trust in God we are perpetually moving "into" Christ. I'm pushing against the idea that salvation is a static experience. I believe that Scripture supports the notion that salvation is always unfolding, as it is not destination based but an ever-evolving process. The word *in* seems to connote finality, whereas *into* connotes movement.

inator, designer, creator of life, and humanity. When we trust *into* Jesus, we trust God as Jesus did, through which we are recreated into him (the Logos, the universal Christ), which is the very design for our lives from the beginning. This isn't about believing to go to heaven; it's about trusting to become fully human and participate in re-creating human culture in a way that produces life for all. This is what is meant by "being saved" (*sōzō*). It means to restore humanity to wholeness that includes all, every single one, living in intimate relationship with God and one another. The idea of individual salvation ("I believe so that I go to heaven") would have been anathema to the author of the Fourth Gospel. Salvation is the rebirth of humanity into the divine design from the beginning in which all are loved and included; all hierarchy, violence, and division is destroyed; and all are blessed with abundant life (John 10:10).

This, then, directly affects how we interpret John 3:18–21 regarding the issue of condemnation.

> The one trusting into him is not condemned [*krinetai*], the one not trusting is condemned already, because he has not trusted into the name of the one-of-a-kind son of God. This is the judgment [*krisis*] because the light shined into the human culture and the human beings loved darkness more than the light, for their deeds were evil. For everyone who does evil hates the light and does not come toward the light, in order that his deeds might not be exposed. But the one who does the truth comes toward the light, in order that his deeds be revealed because in God his deeds are done. (my translation)

Note that the Greek verb *krinetai* in verse 18, meaning "is condemned," is related to the verb *krisis*, meaning "judgment." It's from *krisis* that we get the English word *crisis*. This is critical to understanding the concepts of judgment and condemnation in the Fourth Gospel. The author does not make the case that God is a judge sitting on a bench weighing the good against the evil for each person (which is often the concept generated by the popular interpretation of these verses). The reality is that when we choose to live outside our true identity and purpose as children of God, we necessarily find ourselves in crisis, which is God's judgment. Think of a dolphin trying to fly or a labrador retriever refusing to fetch. When we live outside our divinely created identity and purpose, we are like fish out of water, attempting to live in ways that are extraneous to our nature. God doesn't have to judge or condemn us; we create the conditions of crisis and do it to ourselves! Jesus didn't come to condemn us, as verse 17 states, but to save us from ourselves and return us to wholeness through relationship with God and one another.

How we interpret and convey Scripture matters because it informs the culture we seek to create. When our goal is to teach people to "believe in" Jesus so that they don't go to hell when they die, we necessarily create a culture grounded in fear and exclusion. When, however, we can demonstrate through Scripture that Jesus and his followers were more concerned about drawing people into a way of life that produces life for all, we are on the path to creating a culture of love and inclusion. Our goal should not to be teach belief systems. Our goal is to draw people into real life by living as the children of God we're created to be. An effective pathway for such transformation occurs when we as the church guide people into contemplative practices regarding their life experiences to discern God's presence and resulting in active participation in God's mission of restoration and recreation. At Abiding Hope, we call this process contemplation and engagement.

Contemplation and Engagement within the Congregation

Heath, of Duke Divinity School and the Missional Wisdom Foundation, was one of the keynote speakers at the 2017 ELCA Larger Church conference event and shared with our group the call to contemplation and engagement. She provided us with a system for participating in this process:

1. Be fully present to self and context.

2. What am I feeling?

3. What is happening in my life?

4. What is happening in my community?

5. What is happening in the world?

6. Discern where and how God is showing up.

7. How am I experiencing God in my life?

8. How am I experiencing God in the world?

9. What is God working to do in my life or in the world?

10. Make a decision to participate in God's activity.

11. What can I do to support God's work?

12. What are my particular gifts/passions that I can draw upon in service of God's mission in this time and place?

13. Surrender all outcomes to God.

14. Not my will but yours be done.

15. The outcome is not ours to control, that's God's business.

You can see the focus on experience as the foundation for Elaine's system of contemplation and engagement. At no point are we seeking understanding or comprehension. On the contrary, the goal is to be in touch with what we're experiencing through our physical senses, relationships, and spirituality. Once we're in touch with our self and our context, then we begin to discern the many ways in which God is showing up in our lives. Perhaps you have an addiction that God continually seeks to address. Or maybe there is a situation in your community involving young people toward which God continually calls for your participation. Maybe stories of extreme poverty in a place such as Haiti continually touch your heart and call you to action. God can show up in a myriad of ways. The question is: Are we paying attention, and do we have a lens or an ear to recognize God's beckoning when it occurs? This process of contemplation is intended to help us get in touch with ourselves, our context, and God so that we can discern what God is calling us to do.

Contemplation then leads to engagement, to participating in God's activity. If God is calling you to address an addiction, what steps will you take to do so? If you're being called to serve in the community or around the world, how will you do that? It's important that we understand the gifts and passions that we bring to the table so that we can maximize our efforts. None of us possesses gifts for everything, and we know that when we engage in things that don't align with our gift set or deep passions, we create a high potential for burnout. Therefore, we need also to discern our gifts and passions so that we can then discover how best to maximize them in service of God's call. Once we ascertain the call in alignment with our gifts, it's simply a matter of going to work doing, giving, and serving in the manner that we've been called.

The steps of contemplation and engagement (including surrendering all outcomes to God) is probably the most difficult because many of us have a hard time relinquishing control. We want to know that our actions will bear fruit. We want to be able to measure the outcomes. And certainly, metrics of this sort can be extremely valuable. However, if our call is to reduce the rate of suicide among teens or address the extreme poverty in Haiti, there will be moments when it feels like the hill we're climbing is far too steep and insurmountable. But it's up to God to determine how and when suicide or poverty will be eradicated. Our call is to pour ourselves out in service of God, others, and creation. We must trust that our work is not in vain, that God has called other workers to come alongside us and to work parallel to us so that our small contributions are part of a greater, Spirit-driven mission to God's glory. Thus, we serve willingly and generously, surrendering all outcomes to God, recognizing that the journey is as important as the destination.

A couple of years ago at Abiding Hope, we sought to incorporate this system of contemplation and engagement into every aspect of our life together: worship, small groups, children and youth ministries, spiritual formation opportunities, generosity, outreach, and leadership development. We found that it was easiest to engage small groups in this contemplative work, as long as we had clear guiding questions to direct the conversation. Where small groups required assistance was on the engagement side of things. They interpreted engagement as going out to do a service project together. Of course, we encourage and support service projects. However, our aim was to have individuals and groups discern how they were being called to participate in God's activity every day, not just once a quarter. We wanted our groups to discern how God was calling them to serve at home, work, school, neighborhood, and beyond. We found it necessary to be precise with asking questions. How is God showing up in my marriage? How am I being called to use my gifts with my spouse and kids? Or, How is God showing up in my workplace? How am I being called to use my gifts with my coworkers or company? Or, How is God showing up in my neighborhood? How am I being called to be a child of God to my neighbors? By framing the questions this way, we found that people thought less about doing projects and began to concentrate more on living within all contexts as children of God.

We were also intentional about integrating contemplation and engagement into our worship life. Our approach was multifaceted. We redesigned the cards in the pew racks to be less about getting vital information from people to instead asking direct questions for reflection, such as, Where did you see God this week? and, How are you experiencing God in this worship service? As responses roll in each week, we put several of the responses from the previous week (anonymously, of course) on the worship screens, intermingled with the announcements that scroll before the worship service begins. We found that reading what others had written last week helped people with their own discernment for how they were experiencing God themselves.

We also created a "contemplation station" at a location in our worship center that people could approach before or after worship, sometimes following the sermon, or during Communion. The contemplation station changes with each worship series but always involves some basic contemplative questions, which people write down answers to, either leaving them at the station or taking their answers home. Sometimes we don't use a contemplation station but simply invite people to remain in their seats following the sermon to reflect on their experience, guided by questions on the screens.

During Lent 2019 we created a trash heap in the front of the worship center to the left of the altar. During the sermon, people were asked to think of something that they needed to let go of and something else that they needed to take up. Following the sermon, as quiet music played, people were invited to approach the contemplation station to write down what they were letting go, crinkle that paper in their hand, and throw it into the trash heap. On a separate piece of paper, people were asked to write down what they were taking up and then take that paper home to put on their bathroom mirror as a daily reminder. As an example, someone might write that they are letting go of "greed" and throw that into the trash heap. They then write on the other paper "generosity" as the thing they are taking up, then put it on their bathroom mirror to remind themselves each day to be generous with their resources, their time, their love, their forgiveness, their patience. Each week through the series, we focused on different aspects of letting go and taking up so that people weren't doing the exact same exercise each week. We received loads of positive responses and witnessed a tremendous amount of emotion during that Lenten season. When we can get people to emote, we're on the right track, as our emotions are more about heart than head and often the beginning step toward a transformation that leads to life-giving action.

A Personal Story

Several years ago while participating in a poker game with some men who live on my street (none of whom participate in a church), I looked at one of the guys and asked, "How are you doing?" He responded the way most do, "Good. I'm doing good." Sensing some level of sadness or emotional disturbance in my friend, I paused and said, "No, really. How are you?" He put his cards down, sat back, looked me square in the eye, and said, "Preacher, do you really want to know how I'm doing?" I nodded without breaking eye contact. The nearly fifty-year-old husband and father of two said, "I come home from work each day, sit in the chair in my living room, and cry for about thirty minutes."

Everyone at the poker table fell silent as we stared at our friend. We each knew exactly what he was talking about, but none of us had the guts to say it, nor did we have the words to offer our friend to make him better. We each knew the pain, the pressures, the fear, the uncertainty of doing life in this materialistic, suburban context. While the phenomenon of quiet desperation may not be all that new, what was new was that someone actually named it, pointed to it, and made us all look at it. In that moment, we had no idea what to do with it.

From its inception, the church is called to be the alternate community where human beings can honestly point to the disease of our culture and be drawn into a vision for a new way of being. As church participation declined, congregations became more and more driven by the growing individualism and consumerism of the American culture and sought to commodify themselves through programmatic development to become more attractive to the populace. Now that the boomer, generation X, and millennial generations have identified this recent depiction of the church as shallow and inauthentic, the church finds itself at a loss for defining its true identity and calling. Many in the church exhibit knee-jerk reactions to fixing the church by adjusting this, adding that, reorganizing here, and reprogramming there. But the church does not need to be fixed, nor does it need new programs. The goal is life—real, whole, complete life. We in the church are called to create a congregational culture conducive to forming people to live fully as children of God. Through immersion into this culture and with such tools as contemplation and engagement, we are equipped to participate in God's restorative activity of drawing all into oneness with God, others, and creation.

I and my fellow poker players realized that all of us needed more than a monthly poker game. We needed to go deeper with one another, talking about life, talking about our struggles, getting beyond ourselves and our personal anguish. As a result, we began to make time to get together to go for walks, to sit on our decks, and to talk about our marriages, our jobs, our kids. At first it was awkward, as our pride often limited our ability to be vulnerable with one another. After some time, we were able to get better at reaching out to one another, opening up to one another, and sharing life together. While none of the guys in my group are what I would call active church members, our relationship has evolved into the sort of community that Jesus envisioned and modeled for all. This is the restorative and life-giving work that the church is called to lead for the sake of the world. The next chapter will explore Abiding Hope's story in pursuit of becoming such a congregation.

ABIDING HOPE'S STORY

———————

For me, becoming isn't about arriving somewhere or achieving a
certain aim. I see it instead as forward motion, a means of evolv-
ing, a way to reach continuously toward a better self.
The journey doesn't end.

—Michelle Obama, *Becoming*

I have been blessed to serve at Abiding Hope Church (we took
"Lutheran" out of our name about five years ago, which I'll
address later) since 2004. Abiding Hope has an interesting story
that serves as an example for intentional cultural awareness and
development. The congregation was founded in 1987 as a mission start of the American Lutheran Church.[1] Abiding Hope

———

1. The American Lutheran Church, Lutheran Church in America, and Association for Evangelical Lutheran Churches voted to merge in 1987 to form the
ELCA, which started operating in 1988.

resides in unincorporated Jefferson County in a southwestern suburb of Denver. While our address is Littleton, Colorado, there's actually no town or community center in our area. The church facility is surrounded by several neighborhoods protected by homeowner associations, with a variety of shopping plazas and restaurants scattered here and there.

In 1987, when Abiding Hope was founded, many of these neighborhoods did not exist, but it was clear that development was on the way. The founding pastor, Chris Brekke, did an outstanding job in completing the first phase of the building and assembling a strong group of people who were not afraid to take risks and work toward development. Chris served Abiding Hope for five years before departing for another call. He was well aware of the growth and development of the community and discerned that the congregation would best be served by someone with different gifts and skills than he possessed. I was told by some that Chris had said upon his departure, "I'm an obstetrician. I know how to birth a congregation. Abiding Hope now needs a pediatrician, someone who can raise it up." (Chris has told me that while he doesn't remember saying this exactly, the point is certainly true.) I applaud Chris for his self-awareness, his cultural awareness, and frankly, his humility, which enabled him to take another call so that Abiding Hope could find that pediatrician.

That person, the second pastor to serve at Abiding Hope, was Rick Barger. Rick arrived in 1993 after serving four years on the west coast of Florida. Rick brought with him a unique skill set that turned out to be the exact formula needed to develop a healthy, vitalized congregation in a rapidly growing suburban community. Rick, a second-career pastor, was formerly an engineer with a graduate business degree who served as the CEO of a large, family-owned, international construction company.

He came to Abiding Hope with high organizational intelligence (although that term was not known at the time) and strong leadership skills, coupled with dynamic gifts for preaching and teaching. Abiding Hope grew dramatically during the first two years of Rick's ministry, requiring immediate facility expansion. Being a former construction guy, Rick went to work with the leadership of the congregation to design and build a new worship center that could seat 650 along with an expanded administration wing to provide office space for the growing staff. The new building project was completed in 1997, just four years after Rick's arrival. The congregation became recognized as one of the fastest growing and larger congregations of the ELCA.

A significant factor in the growth of the congregation was the culture that Rick and the leaders had created.[2] Based on my personal experience with Rick's leadership at Abiding Hope, some key aspects of the cultural development were:

- **Clearly focusing on worship, relationships, service, and generosity:** Rick knew intuitively that the mission of the congregation was to transform lives and that the path to transformation was to get people to step out of themselves in love and service toward God and neighbor. Rick viewed worship as the primary means for enculturating people into the Jesus way of life. This then was lived out through relationships, service, and generosity.

- **Emphasizing that all means *all*, and the gifts of God are free:** What people notice most about Abiding Hope is the radically inclusive culture, in which all are welcomed and loved. Statements are made every week before Holy Communion is served to make a clear

---

2. In order to get a full sense for the culture of Abiding Hope under the leadership of Rick Barger, read his book, *A New and Right Spirit.*

point that all are invited to participate. Because of this radically inclusive component within the Abiding Hope culture, there were no waves during the ELCA's discernment and decision regarding human sexuality. In 2009, when the ELCA made the decision to permit the ordination of persons who identify as LGBTQ, Abiding Hope members simply said, "That makes sense because the gifts of God are free!"

- **Giving little attention to being "Lutheran"**: At Abiding Hope, living as children of God is our primary identity and call. Rick used to say, "I bet half of the people at Abiding Hope don't even know that we're Lutheran."

- **Giving permission**: People were given blanket permission to do ministry. Teams did not need to seek approval from the council to create ministries.

- **Eliminating voting**: The congregation conducts one vote each year at the annual gathering to approve the mission spend plan, the slate of leaders, and any other constitutionally mandated items. All other decisions are made through conversation and consensus. Rick understood that voting is inherently divisive and wanted to avoid such issues. He often said, "Robert's Rules of Order and constitutions are not in Scripture." Rick's sense was that if people could not agree on a decision, then more conversation and discernment needed to happen.

- **Moving from budget to mission spend plan**: Very often congregations figure out how much money they think they can raise in a year and then create a budget for how those funds will be expensed. Rick and the leaders did the opposite. They prayed and discerned what ministries God was calling the congregation to conduct in the next year, figured out what that would cost, and then went to the congregation to ask for the funds to achieve the mission set before them.

- **Abolishing endowments and trust funds:** Abiding Hope became one of the most generous congregations in the ELCA, giving away between 30 and 40 percent of income to ministries beyond our doors. Rick was always quick to refer to Jesus in Luke 12:16–34, saying, "Do not build bigger barns or storehouse wealth." Rick would say, "There are people hungry today, naked today, hurting today. They can't wait for us to balance our budget and build up a reserve before we help them. They need our help. God needs our help right now."

- **Creating opportunities for relational service:** Sometimes congregations engage in service projects that tend to be transactional, meaning that the congregants go somewhere to do something for someone without building ongoing relationships. The culture of Abiding Hope was formed around the accompaniment model of service, which starts first with relationship and listening, which then leads to working together so that both the servant and the one being served benefit mutually.

In 2003, the third and final building phase of Abiding Hope was completed, which was the addition of a discipleship training center intended to serve the youth and families of our community in response to the Columbine shooting of 1999. With this addition, all three acres were fully utilized, with no possibility for future building expansion. In 2006, the leadership began to discern possibilities for how best to continue to advance the mission of Abiding Hope. In 2007, a second worshipping site was launched, in an elementary school about twenty-five minutes (fifteen miles) from Abiding Hope's main campus in an area of new and rapid suburban development. The second campus grew quickly, using the same cultural components that had built Abiding Hope's main campus. In 2008, Rick accepted another call and departed Abiding Hope. His new congregation (Epiphany, in Suwanee, Georgia) adopted the same values and culture of Abiding Hope, and the two congregations became partners in our work in Haiti. Even though Rick no longer serves in Suwanee, Abiding Hope and Epiphany continue to be missional partners.

In April 2009, the leadership adopted a three-person lead-team model instead of calling a single lead pastor. Chad Johnson, Glenn Hecox, and I had been working together since 2004 under Rick's leadership and began to live into this new model. Having a triad leading a large and growing congregation versus a single lead pastor certainly has presented challenges, but for the most part this model worked in helping the congregation to transition from the leadership of a strong, dynamic lead pastor. It's not uncommon for congregations to struggle after the end of a long-term pastorate. However, the congregational culture that Rick created was far more focused on the culture of mission than on any single personality. Abiding Hope continued to thrive. The lead team model continued through 2016, at which time Chad Johnson accepted another call, and the leaders made the decision to return to a traditional lead pastor model, identifying me as the sole lead pastor. This has remained our model since.

Discerning the Best Way to Be a Blessing

In 2012, the bishop of the Rocky Mountain Synod approached us about the possibility of releasing our second campus to become an independent congregation, with the caveat that it relocate about seven miles farther south in a bedroom community called Castle Pines, Colorado. The reason for the request was that the ELCA congregation in Castle Rock had chosen to leave the ELCA following the denomination's 2009 decision regarding human sexuality, and a group of people wished to remain in the ELCA and needed a congregation. At the time, the synod was not in a position to be able to launch a new congregation in Castle Rock, and so Abiding Hope agreed to release the second site, and the congregation moved farther south. The congregation was named Well of Hope and became a congregation under development for the ELCA.

In hindsight, it was a poor decision to move to Castle Pines. Castle Pines is a very wealthy area, with a median household income of over $160,000 per year. Most of the neighborhoods are gated, and it's difficult to get the attention of the residents. In addition, we learned that many of the people who had been attending worship in the elementary school location had no desire to drive seven miles south each week. Furthermore, many of the people in Castle Rock who desired to remain in the ELCA did not want to drive seven miles north to attend worship. While the decision looked like a sweet compromise at first, it turned out to be a very bad decision all around. The synod called a young, newly ordained pastor directly out of seminary to serve at Well of Hope. She was placed into a very difficult setting and received very little support. The synodical structure at the time assigned a single synod staff person, who was responsible for supervising all the congregations that were under development or redevelopment. It's a hugely inefficient system that has consistently proven not to work. Aside from providing funding, Abiding Hope was kept at arm's length and was strongly deterred from interfering in any way with Well of Hope. As a result, Well of Hope atrophied rapidly, and the young pastor departed for another call within about three years.

The story of Well of Hope serves as an example for how a ministry or congregation can become derailed when it loses its focus on cultural architecture and does not have support from a vitalized congregation. In retrospect, the congregation should have remained in its original location, and if going independent would have benefited from an ongoing accompaniment partnership with Abiding Hope. We could have created a covenant to define the necessary boundaries. Hopefully in the future judicatories will be proactive in advocating for such relationships between newly developing congregations and vitalized congregations.

With the release of Well of Hope, the leaders of Abiding Hope were again tasked with creating a vision for ongoing development. The options considered during the discernment process were:

1. Change nothing. Just keep going forward doing ministry on our current campus.

2. Launch another second site in a different community.

3. Sell the current campus and purchase ten to fifteen acres nearby to grow and expand the congregation.

4. Come alongside struggling congregations in areas of high potential for congregational development and help them to revitalize.

After a great deal of study and conversation, the leadership and the congregation voted unanimously for the fourth option. The reasoning behind choosing this option was built entirely out of the Abiding Hope culture of service and generosity. The research conducted by the leaders during the discernment process identified the steady decline of congregations in the ELCA. We estimated that 85 to 90 percent of ELCA congregations were either stuck or declining. Fewer persons were entering ministry, which was creating a clergy gap, making it increasingly difficult for congregations to find and call pastors. According to the ELCA Division for Research and Evaluation, the clergy gap is currently about one thousand and will reach two thousand by 2026 (meaning that there will be two thousand ELCA congregations looking for a pastor but won't be able to find one). Another staggering piece of data is that the median worship attendance for ELCA congregations in 2016 was seventy. In 2017, the number declined to sixty-six. I anticipate that when the 2018 numbers are published, they will reveal the median worship attendance to have dipped close to sixty. A congregation that has sixty people or fewer at worship per week is not sustainable long-term.

Data such as these were very concerning to the Abiding Hope leaders, resulting in a unanimous decision to do something that would aid in revitalization for congregations, synods, and our denomination. The Abiding Hope "Generous Life Vision" was adopted in 2014 and began to be implemented in 2015 (see appendix A). The key components to the Generous Life Vision are:

1. Increase our missional effectiveness.

2. Remain true north biblically and theologically, boldly broadcasting our unique message while continually demonstrating that all means *all*.

3. Weave individual stories into God's story to form identity and purpose.

4. Inspire the Abiding Hope community to be consistently in worship, building relationships, involved in service, and practicing radical generosity.

5. Unite others to work as one in serving the world.

6. Partner with churches at risk of closing to raise them up again.

7. Explore possibilities for creating worship and ministries that serve the growing Latino population of the Denver community.

8. Expand our outreach and service both locally and globally.

9. Be a blessing to the greater church.

10. Establish an Abiding Hope leadership network.

11. Create a publishing house to provide resources for other leaders, congregations, and organizations.

12. Seek partnerships with diverse organizations that share a vision for the greater good.

The necessary first step in implementing the Generous Life Vision was to raise additional funds to increase the staff size to meet the demands of the new vision and to support the development of the congregation. The initial Generous Life appeal was conducted in 2015, with commitments for 2016 to 2018. We currently conduct a Generous Life appeal every two years on the even-numbered years as we continue living into the vision. In 2016, we approached the bishop and director for evangelical mission for the Rocky Mountain Synod to share the Generous Life Vision and to ask for their support in identifying three congregations that would benefit from a partnership with Abiding Hope. The synod leadership identified three congregations and assisted us in making the initial contacts and then discerning with each congregation what a partnership might look like. The relationship with each congregation is unique because the needs of each congregation are different.

Accompanying Partner Congregations

We call our system the accompaniment model, which mirrors the way that we have been doing outreach throughout the history of Abiding Hope. The accompaniment model derives directly from the Abiding Hope culture of relational service. We don't come to the table as the experts who bring all the answers. We come as brothers and sisters to hear and learn about the struggles our congregational partners are facing, to offer our knowledge and experience with cultural awareness and organizational intelligence as we work together to discern the path forward. Such relationship development and trust building takes time.

When we first approached the synod leadership with the Generous Life Vision, the director for evangelical mission asked, "How is it going to feel to the people of the struggling congregation when you reach out to them? It's going to be like a battleship pulling alongside a dinghy." I was infuriated when I heard this. My initial reaction was to think, "Battleship? You perceive our congregation to be a battleship outfitted with enormous guns and weapons intending to blow other congregations out of the water?" I was angry. But I soon discovered she was correct. That's exactly the initial reaction of these struggling congregations.

It's critically important that we who seek to serve and to partner recognize the realities that the struggling congregations have been facing over long periods of time. They have been discerning whether to close or remain open because none of the changes or new initiatives they've attempted in the past ten to twenty years have worked in generating revitalization. They've watched pastors come and go. Just paying the bills has gotten to be more and more difficult. They're tired. They're scared. Long-term members of such a congregation know it as the place where they were married, where their kids were baptized, where their parents' funerals were conducted, and now it is fading away and they can't stop the decline. They have already begun to grieve and to accept the apparently unavoidable reality that their beloved congregation is going to close. Now a big, successful congregation is showing interest. Why? Isn't it obvious? The big church wants to swallow up and take over the dying church, which means that the voices of the people in the struggling church will be disregarded and their views and opinions won't matter. Everything they have known and loved about church will suddenly go away.

I was largely naive to the emotional realities of those in a struggling congregation, but when I experienced it firsthand, my initial reaction was to have deep compassion. Meeting the people of the potential partner congregations and experiencing their pain reminded me of the story of Mark 6:34, in which Jesus comes ashore and sees the crowds and "had compassion for them, because they were like sheep without a shepherd." The Greek word that is often translated as "compassion" is *splagchnizomai*. This unique Greek verb derives from the noun *splagchnon*, which means "inward parts" or "of the gut." In other words, what Jesus felt when he came ashore was like a blow to the gut. Jesus has a powerful, visceral reaction seeing the pain and suffering of others, which triggers immediate action on his part. The passage continues by saying that Jesus "began to teach them many things."

I found that before we could begin teaching many things, we

needed to build the trust to alleviate the fear. We needed to assure the people that the congregation was still theirs. We were simply coming as brothers and sisters to walk alongside them. How we went about doing this was different in each of the three partnerships. The three congregations that the synod leadership recommended for partnership were (1) Christ the King, Denver, Colorado; (2) Rejoice, Erie, Colorado; and (3) Well of Hope, Castle Rock, Colorado.

It made sense that Well of Hope would be one of our congregational partners, as we already had a relationship and were still supporting the congregation financially. As stated above, Well of Hope had struggled after becoming an independent congregation under development and moving farther south. The departure of the first pastor now afforded the synod and the small group of about thirty people at Well of Hope the opportunity to think critically about their congregation. Everything was on the table. Should they close, move again, become a satellite of another congregation? What would be the best option for the future? As Well of Hope still maintained the status of being a congregation under development, the synod council was responsible for identifying and calling the new pastor. After a great deal of conversation, Julie McNitt was called to serve as the new pastor at Well of Hope.

Julie and her family had been members of Abiding Hope for the previous few years while she had been on leave from call to focus her attention on her young family. Julie was now ready to return to parish ministry, and this arrangement appeared to be a perfect fit. Julie began to engage the people of Well of Hope into conversation about moving the congregation down to Castle Rock, a growing community with far more potential for congregational development than Castle Pines. They identified a storefront in an excellent location and signed a lease. Abiding Hope provided funding to purchase chairs and help with the renovations in transforming the former fitness center into a worship space. Julie's family lives in a neighborhood near Abiding Hope (about thirty miles north of Castle Rock), so we provide Julie office space and assistance when necessary. She has access to our staff and office equipment, which saves on expenses for Well of Hope. She and I talk periodically about ministry strategy, and we are the first place she turns when needing any form of assistance. Our two congregations share in a few joint ministry ventures, such as our annual thanksgiving basket appeal, and Abiding Hope continues to provide $20,000 of annual financial support. Since the move to Castle Rock, Well of Hope is once again growing and doing well. Our partnership will continue until Well of Hope can truly become fully independent.

The Work of Vitalization Often Includes Struggle

I have learned a great deal from our experience of accompanying struggling congregations toward revitalization. The following sections might feel a bit harsh as I write about behaviors that we experienced that negatively affect congregational development. I am sharing these stories because I believe they exemplify the realities that a high percentage of first-call pastors face when called into a struggling congregation. I have done my best to protect the identities of persons, as I do not want to shame or embarrass anyone. However, I hope that addressing each case will be a blessing to others who find themselves in similar situations.

The partnership with Rejoice in Erie, Colorado, is significantly different from our relationship with Well of Hope. Erie, located directly north of Denver, about fifty miles from Abiding Hope, is the fastest-growing community in Colorado (which says a lot, since Colorado is one of the top five fastest-growing states in the country). However, Rejoice is not near the heart of the growth. In fact, the facility is located on a dead-end dirt road, looks like a log house, and does not have any signage from the main roads because community ordinances do not permit them.

The first time I visited Rejoice, I had a very difficult time finding the church even with the use of GPS. In conversation with the synod's director for evangelical mission, she told me that part of my role in working with Rejoice was to raise the question about relocating to a part of Erie with more potential for development. I quickly learned that the people of Rejoice had a deep, emotional connection to their current facility. Relocating was not on the table. It turned out that IKEA and some other businesses were about to build on the land surrounding Rejoice, and the members were certain that the sprawl of development would soon reach their current location.

Another challenge was that the congregational culture was very "pastor-centered," meaning that the members expected the pastor to know all their names and to have a personal relationship with them. She was expected to greet every child by name before each children's message. She personally visited each family that attended worship for the first time. No decisions in the congregation were made without her involvement. As a congregation grows, it becomes impossible for the pastor to know everyone's name, to visit everyone who attends worship for the first time, and to be involved in every decision made within the congregation. Under these sorts of expectations and long-term practice, such a culture becomes entrenched, difficult to change, and a road-block to development. It was clear to me that even if Rejoice were to relocate to an area of great potential for development, it still would not become vitalized under the current culture. A lot would need to be changed.

Rejoice had reached a point where it could not pay its bills and struggled financially. It was in arrears on mortgage payments, even after moving to an interest-only payment plan. The pastor reported to me that often her paycheck was late. The congregation's financial situation created a great deal of stress among the leadership, which ultimately resulted in leaders turning on one another.

When we first engaged with Rejoice, I discovered there was a measure of toxic behavior among the leadership. The president of the congregation, a very good man with an enormous heart, was exhausted and out of options for how best to lead. A member of council had recently made a surprise motion at a council meeting to fire the pastor. Upon learning about this incident, I contacted the director for evangelical mission at the synod office to inform her of what had transpired and to discern a path forward. We decided that it would be best for me and a couple of our Abiding Hope leaders to meet directly with the council at Rejoice to define some boundaries.

The first boundary was that gossiping to create a coalition against the pastor would not be tolerated. Every congregational leader had to demonstrate healthy behavior, especially when addressing conflict. If there was a problem with the pastor's leadership, then we would create appropriate processes and systems to address it. Our team pointed out the destructive effects of blindsiding one another at meetings. The woman who had made the surprise motion to fire the pastor asked whether she could speak with me privately. I consented but made it clear that I was the wrong person to be trying to coerce and manipulate the pastor. My job as a congregational partner to Rejoice was not to evaluate or remove the pastor but to serve as a coach and mentor for the pastor and the congregational leaders. I informed her that this would be the last conversation that she and I would have regarding the performance of the pastor and that she needed to either get on board with the rest of the council or step down. Within the next week, she resigned from the council and left the congregation. No other persons followed her.

Some at Rejoice felt a sense of relief when the disgruntled council member departed, but I knew that we had simply dipped a toe into the turbulent waters. It was clear that Rejoice had no vision for where to go or what to do. It lacked guiding statements, had no sense of identity or purpose, and was largely driven by opinion. Without a clear sense of congregational identity or purpose, decisions fall to individual opinions or preferences. This necessarily results in division as people don't often agree on what they like or want. Often congregations without clarity of identity or purpose adopt a mindset of scarcity as they worry about money, the lack of members, or who gets to make the decisions. The fear associated with such a mindset is crippling and greatly inhibits the congregation's ability to think and act creatively or to take necessary risks. The remedy is to create clear and compelling guiding statements upon which a healthy, vitalized culture can be created.

The first thing we did was to assemble a vision team separate from the council that would be tasked with leading the congregation through a series of gatherings to engage members in conversation toward the goal of creating guiding statements: vision, mission, core values, tagline (see chap. 3). I also began to work with the congregation president on creating agendas and establishing clear role definitions for the council. I met with the pastor periodically to listen and to coach, and I attended every vision team meeting.

Once in a while, persons from the Rejoice council or vision team would make the forty-five-minute drive down to Abiding Hope to attend a worship service. We also hosted a few of the

Rejoice vision team meetings at Abiding Hope as an aspect of our partnership. Although Abiding Hope did not provide any financial support for Rejoice, we permitted Rejoice to access our staff and leaders. For instance, our lead servant for resources helped Rejoice to create a new spend plan and financial reporting system. We also aided Rejoice in accurately reporting congregational data to the synod and the mission investment fund.

The bulk of our work throughout the first eighteen months was to aid Rejoice in the creation of guiding statements. Once the guiding statements were created and approved by the congregation, we then moved into the strategic planning phase. This is where things bogged down, as is common in the revitalization process. The system we use for constructing a strategic plan (see chap. 4) is built from the core values identified in the guiding statements. Remember that the primary goal is not to generate programs or ministries but to create a culture into and through which people will be immersed and transformed. This isn't easy work and is especially difficult for someone who has little or no experience in cultural and strategic development.

Because of unexpected health issues, the pastor retired and the congregation was placed back on mission status by the synod. The synod council called and assigned a pastor to Rejoice for three years with the sole intent of continuing the congregation's movement toward revitalization. I and Abiding Hope continue to accompany Rejoice in the process of strategic cultural development, and we are hopeful that the Spirit will create new opportunities for mission and ministry. Concurrent with the pastoral change at Rejoice, our synod also called a new Director for Evangelical Mission. Building new relationships takes time, but I am confident that we all share a passion for seeing Rejoice become a fully vitalized congregation who will eventually pay it forward by accompanying other congregations in their cultural development.

Abiding Hope's partnership with Christ the King, Denver, is by far the most involved of the three partnerships. Of the three partners, Christ the King exhibited the most reticence and fear in working with us. Christ the King was founded in 1956 as a congregation of the American Lutheran Church in what was the first wave of housing development southwest of urban Denver, in a community known as Harvey Park. Most of the houses in the neighborhood were built by families from the upper Midwest who had come to Denver with their GI bills and government funding. Coming from the upper Midwest, many of these families were of German or Scandinavian descent, meaning many had roots in a Lutheran congregation. Records indicate that within eighteen months from its point of organization, Christ the King had grown to having more than one thousand members. Christ the King grew to be one of the largest congregations in the synod, until in the 1970s things began to change.

Latinos began to move into Harvey Park as the whites moved farther away from the urban setting into newly developing suburban communities. Membership at Christ the King began to decline. Christ the King experienced several pastors leaving after only a few years. As the neighborhood changed, attempts at drawing Latinos into worship and membership consistently failed. To be honest, the message the congregation inadvertently sent into the community was: "We'd love for you to come and join us and worship the way we worship, eat the foods that we eat, enjoy the music that we enjoy, and become like us." Very few Latinos showed interest in joining Christ the King. The story of Christ the King is probably like countless other congregations in urban settings around the country. As the neighborhoods change, the congregations don't adapt, and the result is decline and inevitable death.

When we began to engage with Christ the King in mid-2016, it had been having serious conversations about closing. The average worship attendance was about thirty, and the average age of the congregation was eighty-one. It had not had a confirmation class or even a children's message in worship for years. Thanks to a large endowment created from an estate gift, Christ the King did still have a full-time pastor. We discovered that the pastor had been the one leading the conversation about closing, while most in the congregation were not ready to close. As I greeted people following my first experience preaching at Christ the King, an elderly woman squeezed my hand and leaned in close to my face to say, "This congregation will close over my dead body." Those who were still there had a deep love for their congregation and would do anything to preserve it.

We knew that if Abiding Hope was to partner with Christ the King, the pastor would have to leave. The culture had become toxic. The people loved their pastor, but many had lost confidence in his ability to lead them, for they knew he believed they should close. The congregation had elected a woman to be president who had just joined the congregation the month prior. The reason she had been elected president is that people had begun to fear that the congregation was going to close, and no one wanted to be the president who closed it.

To address the leadership issues, the director for evangelical mission and I worked to draft a covenant document that would define the partnership between Abiding Hope and Christ the King. According to that document, the congregation council would be dissolved, and a vision team consisting of four Christ the King members and three Abiding Hope members would be formed. We created the joint vision team because Abiding Hope was temporarily providing the staff leadership for the congregation, and we felt that having three Abiding Hope members on the vision team would help create better connection and synergy between the two congregations. The pastor would be asked to resign, and the synod staff would assist him in finding a new call. He would be provided a generous severance package, and his benefits would be extended for as long as necessary until he received a new call. We had several open-forum conversations with the members of the congregation before they decided to accept the new covenant.

The one person opposing the partnership was the president. Fortunately, she had no supporters within the congregation. Everyone could see that it was a mistake to elect her president; they just didn't know what to do about it. The new partnership was the perfect solution to have her step down from the leadership role. Unfortunately, she did not support the newly forming relationship between Christ the King and Abiding Hope and thus chose to leave the congregation.

With the dissolution of the council and the removal of the pastor, Abiding Hope now bore the responsibility for providing both staff and lay leadership. We needed four Christ the King members to serve on the vision team. When we opened nominations to the congregation, only four people stepped forward willing to serve. People were still quite skeptical that this partnership was going to work, and no one wanted it to be their fault if it failed. Whether they were qualified or not, all four volunteers were appointed to the team. Three strong leaders from Abiding Hope who were committed to the Generous Life Vision were identified, and all three agreed to serve. We knew that to transform the toxic culture at Christ the King, we would first need to build a high level of trust. Making swift and radical changes would not be the best path toward building that necessary trust. Our initial focus rested on just a few key areas: worship, pastoral care, and cultural development.

We wanted to improve the quality of worship immediately by elevating the level of preaching and worship leadership. All the Abiding Hope pastors and pastoral interns (at the time we had three full-time ordained pastors and two pastoral interns) took turns leading worship at Christ the King. Our bishop licensed our pastoral interns to preside at Communion when it was their turn to lead worship at Christ the King. Because this new partnership, as part of our Generous Life Vision, was overwhelmingly approved by the people of Abiding Hope, our congregation was willing to sacrifice a pastoral leader each weekend knowing that we were working to revitalize Christ the King. We publicized which pastoral leader was at Christ the King each week. We found that by making this announcement, some Abiding Hope members would periodically choose to worship at Christ the King as a sign of our solidarity.

A cultural factor within the congregation was that everyone had to participate in every decision. People wanted to know how much money was spent on every item, and any sort of decision-making had to be opened for corporate conversation. There was no trust in the leadership. Leaders were not empowered to lead. Understanding this reality, we chose not to make any other staff changes until greater trust could be established. We realized that making other significant moves before having adequate trust in the leadership would be detrimental to future development. So we chose to make only a few small changes here and there while we worked diligently to build deep relationships and establish a high level of trust.

A key part of our focus was on pastoral care. Christ the King had a sizable number of shut-ins who received regular visits from a committed team of congregational members. Our pastoral team began to work alongside the women who were visiting the shut-ins to provide necessary support and to also visit the homebound. Word spread quickly about the quality of care that the sick and suffering were receiving. This was huge in building the necessary trust capital that would be needed when we began to make significant changes.

Assessing the Congregation's Culture

We worked with the vision team to train the members on cultural development. We helped them to begin to assess the current culture of Christ the King in comparison to the culture of Abiding Hope. It was truly fascinating to watch as people became culturally aware and began to recognize, for the first time, some of the cultural realities that had kept Christ the King stuck and struggling for so long. We introduced the process to create new guiding statements (vision, mission, core values, tagline) that engaged the congregation in conversation and gleaned information that would be necessary for later creating the statements. One of our pastoral interns created a detailed historical telling of the story of Christ the King, paying special attention to historical trends and key pivot points throughout the past sixty years. The telling of the story provided a foundation for the new development that was beginning to take place. In fact, we learned that Christ the King was a key player in the birth of Abiding Hope back in the late 1980s. Christ the King, one of the strongest American Lutheran Church congregations in the area at the time, provided financial support that helped to launch Abiding Hope.

Suddenly, we weren't just two congregations that were choosing to partner. Abiding Hope was the adult child of an aging parent and now bore the responsibility to care for the one who had previously cared for us. This discovery created a deep emotional connection between Abiding Hope and Christ the King. When this story was told at Abiding Hope, people were deeply moved and inspired to participate in and support the partnership. The people at Christ the King suddenly could recall this shared history and no longer saw Abiding Hope as a threat to their autonomy but instead as a gift from God sent to bring new life. The energy had begun to shift from fear to hope.

One of our pastoral interns, Joel Rothe, served with us at Christ the King for two years as he completed his seminary requirements. Following internship, Joel was on track to enter the call process. Joel is in his early thirties and is a second-career pastor. His undergraduate degree is in business, and he possesses amazing leadership skills and strong pastoral instincts. We were using the pastoral interns more and more at Christ the King as the partnership advanced, and it was clear that the people of Christ the King had developed an affinity toward Joel and he toward them. We began to explore the possibility that Joel be called to be the pastor at Christ the King following the completion of his seminary requirements.

Because of the polity of the ELCA, we could not make this decision ourselves. We would need to gain the approval of the bishop, the synod council, and Joel's candidacy team in California. Once we were certain that both Joel and the people of Christ the King were open to the idea (boy, were they excited for this possibility), we approached the bishop, the synod council, and the candidacy team. All gave their approval, and Joel was ordained and installed at Christ the King. The partnership continued according to the covenant arrangement. The joint vision team continued to be the governing body for the congregation, and I continued to serve in a coaching role with Joel.

Ironically, shortly after Joel's installation came our first potentially damaging conflict. I am aware of the sensitivity in sharing this story. I have received permission from the leadership at Christ the King to share this story, as what follows is well-known within the congregation. The reason for sharing is to demonstrate the toxicity of culture and behavior that many first-call pastors must face when called into struggling congregations. My sincere hope is that this can be used as a case study in emotional intelligence as it relates to congregational leadership and vitality.

The woman who had been in charge of the altar guild for more than forty years was causing problems. First of all, she did not allow for new people to join the altar guild, and second, everything had to be done her way. Because we had found that people at Abiding Hope truly appreciate receiving freshly baked bread during Communion instead of wafers, we decided to bring this practice to Christ the King. We discussed this change with the vision team and the worship team before making the change. We quickly learned that the leader of the altar guild (let's call her Stella), who refused to attend the worship team meetings and thus missed the opportunity to discuss the change, did not like this idea because bread makes crumbs that then need to be vacuumed up after worship. Even though the leadership had decided to switch from wafers to bread, Stella consistently refused to provide bread for worship, thus forcing the use of wafers. As stated above, she refused to attend meetings with the worship team because she would not permit anyone to hold her accountable. Finally, her most egregious offense occurred publicly during worship. Shortly after Joel's installation, we had developed the necessary trust capital to dismiss the accompanist/music leader and call an incredibly gifted musician/leader. The new person played the piano with great energy and passion, encouraging congregational singing and participation. Unfortunately, Stella didn't like this one bit. She thought the piano was too loud. She complained frequently about it. We had heard a story of Stella, some years ago, pulling the plug on the organ during a worship service because she thought it was too loud.

On a particular Sunday morning shortly after the arrival of the new musician, Stella left her pew during the first song, approached Joel from behind, smacked him square in the back, and yelled, "THE PIANO IS TOO LOUD!" and then returned to her seat. Joel was shaken by this incident and had a difficult time centering himself to continue with the service. How many young, first-call pastors have been forced to deal with the situation of a difficult member? To exacerbate the situation, we were told by several people at Christ the King, "Do not make Stella angry or else she'll take the stove." Wait a minute . . . what? Apparently, the stove in the kitchen was purchased with memorial funds that were donated to Christ the King in memory of Stella's mother. Since then, any time that Stella felt attacked, she would threaten to leave Christ the King and take the stove with her (which, by the way, was not her stove at all but the property of the congregation). Up to now, everyone had bowed to Stella's manipulation.

Joel and I sat with the vision team to discuss how to address the situation. When one of the Christ the King members said, "You know, she's going to take the stove if you confront her about this," I responded, "I'll help her carry the stove to the curb and load it in her vehicle. We're not going to be held hostage by a stove." The looks on the faces of the vision team members were priceless. You could see instant relief, as though they were thinking, "Right! Why would we be held hostage for a stove? It's just a stove. We need to support our pastor and the development of the congregation." We then identified three members of the vision team (two from Christ the King and one from Abiding Hope) who would accompany Joel and me as we met with Stella. Joel contacted Stella and scheduled the conversation. Joel opened the conversation by thanking Stella for agreeing to talk and then offered a prayer. He then read aloud the core values of the congregation that had been created as part of the guiding statements and asked each person to verbally state whether they supported and would live each value. Once everyone, including Stella, responded affirmatively to the values, I then took leadership of the conversation.

I explained to Stella that what she did to Joel in worship was not acceptable. I asked Joel to describe for Stella what it was like for him to be surprised by a sharp blow to the back followed by a verbal scolding during the worship service. Joel explained how unnerving this was and the difficulty he had in recentering himself to lead worship and to preach. I invited Stella to respond to Joel's comments. She immediately began to defend her opinion that the music was too loud. I interrupted her and asked her to repeat back to Joel what she had heard him say. She obliged me and repeated Joel's sentiments. I asked her whether she could understand why this sort of behavior was problematic and could not be condoned. She said that she could. I then asked her to identify some other, more constructive ways that she could address the situation. She quickly responded that she had talked to Joel and other leaders about the music but no one was doing anything about it. I then asked, "Do the leaders have to do everything you say? What if they don't agree with you? What if the majority of the congregation doesn't agree with you?" I continued, "In fact, we are hearing wonderful and amazing comments regarding the new musician. You're the only person who appears to be upset."

Stella knew this to be true. She was complaining all the time, and no one was agreeing with her. At the same time, no one would set her straight because everyone was afraid of her. I told her that from now on, we expect her to address problems appropriately, through healthy dialogue. If she didn't like the decisions that the leaders were making, she either needed to accept it or she could leave the congregation. I explained to her that none of us wanted that, of course, but that we could not allow toxic behavior to damage the pastor or the congregation.

I then turned the conversation toward the altar guild. I asked Stella how long she had been in charge of the altar guild. She said, "A long time." I told her that as the congregation grew, the demands on the altar guild were going to increase. It would become necessary to add new people to the altar guild as the congregation grew. We pointed out that there were only two women (Stella and one other) who participated with altar guild. I asked Stella whether she would be open to Pastor Joel actively recruiting and adding people to the altar guild. Stella paused and then said, "You know, I'm actually tired of the demands of the altar guild. I can't do it myself anymore. Maybe it's time for someone else to be in charge."

I wasn't sure whether this was a passive-aggressive manipulative ploy or whether she was being sincere and asking for help. After all, it couldn't be easy to be in charge of the altar guild for forty years. Stella was eighty years old, or close to it. Maybe she really was ready to step aside. So I asked, "Would you be willing to help train the people who will replace you?" She answered, "Sure, I can do that." I concluded, "Great! Pastor Joel will enlist some new people to serve on the altar guild, and you will work together to train them and pass the torch. How does that sound?" Stella replied, "That sounds fine." We thanked Stella for the conversation, for hearing Pastor Joel, for helping to find a solution for the altar guild, and for working with us.

We were all shocked, especially the Christ the King vision

team members, at how the conversation played out. Word spread about the amazing job Joel did in addressing Stella, which increased his trust capital in the congregation. Stella is still an active member of Christ the King and no longer complains about the music or tries to sabotage worship. This incident demonstrates a seismic shift in the Christ the King culture that caused people to be less fearful and become more hopeful that God isn't quite done with Christ the King but has big plans for their congregation. However, without the guiding statements and especially the core values, we would not have had a strong enough foundation to address Stella. Guiding statements define the culture and the way of life that we seek to live as God's people. Guiding statements hold us accountable to our identity and purpose. Guiding statements are the first place that we need to start as we assess a current congregational culture and discern the culture to be developed.

It's impossible to script a plan that will work in every situation. However, through taking the time to build trusting relationships, we are able to arrive at a mutual understanding for how best to proceed toward revitalization. But again, this is very hard work. The good news is that there are many tools, along with principles of leadership and organizational intelligence, that can be applied in most every situation. Still, we always need to assess whether the tools we're using are appropriate to the task at hand. The next chapter will outline some of the tools to be used in the process toward revitalization.

3

LAYING THE FOUNDATION FOR TRANSFORMATION

The most difficult project in the world is the re-construction
of the human mind.

—Rev. Dr. Myles Munroe, Bahamian pastor (1954–2014)

Before we dive into processes and procedures for generating
effective guiding statements for a congregation, we need to
engage in an ecclesiological conversation to ascertain the identity and purpose for a church. A congregation, as part of the
church universal, should have a mission that aligns with the *missio Dei*, the mission of God. As children of God, we do not get
to invent our own identity or purpose; both have already been
given to us by the Creator. In baptism we have been claimed,
named, and called to use all our gifts, abilities, and resources in

service of God's mission in the world. As such, we had better have clarity regarding God's mission if we are to identify a congregation's role and participation within God's divine design for humanity and the world.

Russ Crabtree, former lead pastor of a large Presbyterian congregation and founder of Holy Cow Consulting, is a guru on organizational intelligence applied toward congregational development.[1] Crabtree's extensive body of research into why some congregations flourish while most decline (more on this in chap. 4) has identified some promising pathways for congregational development along with several dead ends. Crabtree found that congregations that are clear and undeterred on their theological and ecclesiological grounding tend to have greater success than congregations that try to allow for any and all kinds of thinking. At Abiding Hope, we have spent considerable time and energy to clearly define our theology/ecclesiology and maintain it.[2] Now, I'm not advocating that every congregation must act or think like Abiding Hope. I am choosing to share our ecclesiological framework as an example to aid others in creating such theological clarity.

Our primary hermeneutic at Abiding Hope for scriptural interpretation is what we call a messianic apocalyptic eschatology. This means that we believe that the cosmic Christ (the Logos/Sophia, the Light on day one of the creation, through which all things came into being; see John 1:1–18) was enfleshed in the person of Jesus of Nazareth (Messiah) to reveal (*apokalypsis*) to humanity God's ultimate eschaton, the yet-unfolding

1. Russ Crabtree has several books on the topic of organizational intelligence, including *Owl Sight: Evidence-Based Discernment and the Promise of Organizational Intelligence for Ministry* (St. Louis: Magi Press, 2012); *The State of the Evangelical Lutheran Church in America: An Organizational Intelligence Perspective* (St. Louis: Magi Press, 2016); and *Penguins in the Pews: Climate, Change and Church Growth* (St. Louis: Magi Press, 2017). I highly recommend them all.
2. The Abiding Hope Theology and Ecclesiology is included in the back of this book as appendix B.

vision and divine design for the creation from the beginning of time. What Jesus the Christ reveals to humanity through his life, death, and resurrection is that the *missio Dei* is full communion with all things, that is, that all things dwell and operate within intimate oneness with God and one another.[3]

As we explore Trinitarian theology, specifically the economic Trinity (which focuses on what God does), we discover the workings of God in relationship to the creation. Every aspect of God's being (Father, Son, Holy Spirit) seeks to draw all things into full communion with God and with one another. The church, then, empowered by the Spirit, stands as an extension of the Holy Trinity, serving God's unfolding mission of oneness with all. Therefore, everything we do as church or congregation is to serve the *missio Dei*. The economy of the congregation is both part of and the whole of God's activity within creation. The congregational culture that is to be created through the generation of guiding statements and a strategic plan must also engage a process of discernment using Scripture, congregational history, and the human experience with God and neighbor. Let's explore what such a process could look like.

Creating Guiding Statements

I'm often asked, "How long does it take to create effective guiding statements?" My response is, "That depends." I've seen it done well in as quickly as six months, and I've seen it take more than a year. The average is about nine to twelve months. You don't want to work too quickly, and you don't want to drag it out too long. If you work too quickly, the danger is that you

---

3. For more on this perspective see Karl Rahner, *The Trinity* (New York: Continuum, 2001); Catherine Mowry LaCugna, *God for Us: The Trinity and Christian Life* (San Francisco: HarperSanFrancisco, 1993); and Richard Rohr, *The Universal Christ: How a Forgotten Reality Can Change Everything We See, Hope For, and Believe* (New York: Convergent Books, 2019).

don't engage all the necessary voices in the process, and the results appear to be contrived by a few. If you drag it out too long, you lose momentum because it becomes increasingly difficult to maintain focus. Completing the process within a nine- to twelve-month window is a good target.

Step One: Building the Vision Team

It's important that the team of people assembled to guide a congregation through the process of creating guiding statements, and to wordsmith those new statements, is separate from the top-level governance team or congregation council. It's acceptable to have one member of council serve on the vision team in a liaison role, but we do not want the council to be distracted from its governance duties in order to execute the visioning process. I prefer calling this ad hoc group the vision team because that is exactly what they are doing. They are helping the congregation to gain clarity of vision for identity and purpose. Because the team will be tasked with conducting congregational gatherings, looking through all gathered information, wordsmithing the statements, and disseminating information, it's best to only have about five people plus the pastor(s) on the team. "Too many cooks ruin the soup," my mother used to say, and that will certainly happen if the team is too large.

It's also important that the members of the vision team be big-picture thinkers. When people who tend to be more detail oriented are on the team, they often get frustrated or frustrate the other team members because they skip vision and strategy and move directly to tactical thinking. For example, I was working with a congregation going through a visioning process, and one member of the team kept wanting to talk about Sunday school. She had heard rumors that Sunday school was going away and had asked to be on the team so that she could "protect Sunday school." After several attempts at trying to help her understand that this team was not going to decide whether to keep Sunday school but to create statements that would guide the congregation in all future decision-making, she stepped down from the team, saying, "I don't understand what's going on." Unfortunately, not everyone is visionary and able to see forward. Based on data from Myers-Briggs Type Indicator, a common personality test, only about 25 percent of the population are intuitives (N, people who tend to be more of big-picture thinkers). In my experience, many in leadership within failing congregations lack vision. The church needs people who are gifted for detailed tasks, and thank God for them. However, serving on the vision team requires the gift of vision and discernment. In my experience, there are only a small number of people in the population who possess such gifts.

Another way of looking at things comes from the work of Dr. Everett M. Rogers on how cultural transformation takes place.[4] His S-curve theory related to cultural transformation is regarded highly among scholars and organizational leaders. Rogers's research found that 2.5 percent of the population are what he calls innovators. These are big-picture thinkers who love coming up with new ideas that haven't been explored before. While the innovators are good at coming up with ideas, they aren't always the best ones to implement the new ideas and see them to fruition. That group is called the early adopters. According to Rogers, about 13.5 percent of the population are early adopters. These are people who don't necessarily come up with the new ideas, but they know a good idea when they hear it and have the gifts and abilities to begin to work to bring the ideas to life. Rogers's research indicates that the innovators

4. Everett M. Rogers (1931–2004) was a communication theorist and sociologist at the University of New Mexico and author of *Diffusion of Innovations* (New York: Free Press, 2003). While this seminal work is quite technical in nature, it provides a wealth of information about how to transform culture.

and early adopters combined represent about 16 percent of the population. In a congregation that worships fifty people, who are the eight innovators/early adopters whom you can enlist to build the vision team? That's the group of people you want around the table as you ask questions, glean information, and discern the path forward.

It's also important that the people that you choose to serve on the vision team have strong relationships with others in the congregation so they can influence others when the statements are completed. Rogers identifies the next group in cultural transformation as the early majority. This group makes up about 34 percent of the population. They are the first people, other than the innovators and early adopters, to come on board with new ideas. The reason the early majority aligns with the changes is that they are people who have relationships with the innovators and early adopters. It's not that they can see the new vision clearly or are even excited about the changes, but their friends, whom they trust, are telling them the changes and new vision are a good thing. Therefore, it is important to make sure that those who are called to serve on the vision team are also influencers within the congregation. According to Rogers's research, once the early majority is on board with the new vision, the cultural transformation will happen.

The next group to come on board is what Rogers calls the late majority. This is the 34 percent of the population who lays back to see what everyone else is going to do. Rogers calls the remaining 16 percent of the population the laggards, because they aren't going to accept or adopt the new vision. The congregation will move forward into the transformed culture with or without the laggards. (I'm sure that you can probably name a few of these kinds of folks.) Please don't waste time on bringing the laggards on board. Pastors who have a high need for every-

with this. Once the late majority moves
ft has occurred.

s assembled, it's best to have it ratified
e congregation as an ad hoc team with
. When the vision team completes its
isbanded. A new vision team could be
cessary, and persons from the former
enlisted to serve. However, an ad hoc
ns "for this") should be a temporary
purpose. I have found that people are
serving on a team if it's not a life sen-
l be a lot of work to be done by those
ly be for a short period of time. The
s a member of the team without being
chair of the team. It's important that the congregation trust
that the decisions being made are generated by the team and not
by the pastor alone. Shared decision-making is a better pathway
to congregational support and buy-in.

Step Two: Creating the Culture of the Vision Team

The first and most important aspect of the culture of the vision
team is prayer and Scripture. The team should pray collectively
before each gathering and engage in some form of scriptural
centering led by the pastor. I recommend, during the formation
of the team and the beginning of the visioning process, that
the pastor choose passages from Scripture that speak to the
topics of vision and leadership, aiming toward cultural development to generate a solid foundation for the focus and work
of the team. Some passages I appreciate are Exodus 18; Isaiah
25:6–10a; Jeremiah 1; Matthew 5–7 (the Sermon on the Mount);
Romans 12; 2 Corinthians 5; and Revelation 21:1-7. There are
loads of online tools today that help pastors and leaders find

topical Scripture passages. I have found Bible Gateway, a free resource that includes most Bible translations and is easy to navigate, to be particularly helpful in this regard.[5] Once the team has been established and a solid foundation has been laid, using the Gospel text for the coming weekend as the centering text at each meeting serves to create an immersion into Scripture that goes beyond the meeting itself. After spending about thirty minutes discussing the centering text, the group is then ready to address the work at hand.

In actuality, I begin all meetings (not simply vision team meetings) by centering on Scripture. The reason goes back to the Stephen Covey quotation at the top of chapter 1: "Begin with the end in mind." We do not create the mission of the church. The mission is given to us by God: to draw all into full communion with God, humanity, and creation. However, it's incredibly easy to fall prey to the many tasks at hand within a congregation. It's easy for fear to contaminate our culture as we worry that we don't have enough people or money. Remember that most people are *not* visionary in nature. They struggle to grasp the big picture and remain focused on it, instead preferring to move directly to tactics. I would guess that most congregation council sessions deal less with the big-picture missional direction of the congregation and more with the needed tasks at hand.

By centering every meeting on Scripture, we immerse the participants into the big-picture story of identity and purpose, that is, who we are and why we are here. This centering then prepares us to assess tasks from the perspective of whether they align with the vision and direction of the congregation. The top-level leadership teams should be most concerned with

5. See www.biblegateway.com.

vision and alignment, while allowing ministry teams to concentrate more on details and tactics.

Step Three: Cultural Assessment

A good place to start in becoming culturally aware is to do a demographic study of the greater community surrounding the congregation. Our denomination (ELCA) provides such information free of charge through the synod offices. I don't know whether that's the case for other denominations, but a simple inquiry to your local judicatory can answer that question. If you're looking for other demographic resources, you can check with the local chamber of commerce or your city/county government. A fee-based online resource that I have used multiple times is called Link2Lead, a subsidiary of a product-testing organization called Percept.[6] I have found its demographic information to be quite thorough and informative. Some things to be looking for as you engage in your demographic study are:

- Is the population growing or declining? At what rate per every five years?

- Average age of people

- Generational breakdown (how many millennials, generation X, boomers, etc.)

- Variety and proportions of ethnic groups

- Median household income

- Family structures (single, married, divorced)

- Levels of education

- Primary concerns of the population (What do people need or desire?)

6. See www.link2lead.com.

- Percentage of those affiliated with faith groups versus unaffiliated

- Preferences for worship style (traditional or contemporary)

This information will be valuable as the vision team begins to think about wording the guiding statements, as the statements should be in a language that not only guides the congregation in its cultural development but also speaks to the greater community. It is also worthwhile to do a quick study of the surrounding faith communities. Are other congregations growing or declining? What are some reasons for congregational growth or decline? Is there any wisdom to be gleaned from either their successes or failures? Additionally, if you have a connection with local law enforcement, it's always helpful to have a conversation to see what sorts of things they see in the community that the congregation could address, for example, rising rates of substance abuse, suicide, domestic violence, and so on. Have local schools, therapists, or sociologists conducted research into the social ills of your community? Could you use a sociology professor or student in a nearby college or university to help conduct such a study of your context? The more resources you use in the process, the more accurate picture you will create for the community's cultural realities.

When we began our work with Christ the King (see chap. 2), which sits in a community that is 72 percent Latinx, we engaged local Latinx leaders along with neighbors who live near the congregation to guide us in gathering information from the Latinx community. Prior to our conversations, we assumed that the needs would be English as a second language, tutoring and other assistance for students, and help with documentation/ naturalization. We were utterly shocked to discover that the number-one concern among Latinx families in the neighborhood was keeping families intact. We found that members of the older generation discouraged the youth from going to college for fear that they would get a job elsewhere and move away, leaving no one to care for the grandparents. We also discovered that most of the Latinx households were multigenerational and that the female member of the middle generation often served as both mother to the children and caregiver to the older adults. Very few Latinx families used care facilities for older adults, choosing instead to care for the elderly themselves in their homes. This information dramatically changed the trajectory of our vision for ministry development, as we began to explore creating a drop-in day care center for older adults as a form of respite for overworked and exhausted Latina women.

We had also believed that we would need to incorporate Spanish into our Sunday morning worship to reach the Latinx community. Through our conversations with the community, we discovered that many younger Latinxs had no interest in speaking Spanish. They wanted to speak English, while many older Latinxs only knew Spanish, with very limited English. We decided to keep the Sunday worship service entirely in English, while creating a midweek evening worship experience in Spanish accompanied by a meal. We have found that young Latinx families feel more comfortable worshipping in English on the weekend, while older Latinxs enjoy attending the midweek service in Spanish and receiving a good meal. We would not have come to such conclusions without our vision team reaching out to local Latinx leaders to listen to the true needs and concerns of the community.

Understanding the existing culture, as well as the needs and concerns of the greater context, is critical to the missional success of any congregation, new or established. Jesus often asks people, "What do you want me to do for you?" before healing them (see Matt 20:32, for example). He didn't assume he knew what they needed or wanted. This is a fundamental aspect of accompaniment. It is simply arrogant, hierarchical, and even imperialistic to assume that we know or understand the circumstances of another. Before we can create a vision or plan for how to proceed, we must first build relationships, listen, and then work together in creating the path forward. While we began the community garden at Christ the King (a need that we discovered through the shared dialogue process), it was installed and has been maintained by the entire community, not just the members of Christ the King. The garden serves to provide fresh produce to the neighborhood and is part of a larger network of community gardens throughout the city of Denver. This ministry was initiated and developed through the cultural assessment work conducted by the vision team.

Step Four: Congregational Participation

Early in my ministry, when I was serving in the Southeastern Synod of the ELCA, I was invited to serve on a synodical team tasked with creating new guiding statements for the synod. This team was formed following a disastrous visioning process conducted by the bishop and the synod council. They had created new guiding statements themselves, without engaging congregations and conferences in the process. I must say, the statements they created were pretty good. They would have been effective as the foundation for generating strategic development within the synod. However, when the statements were brought before the annual synod assembly, they failed overwhelmingly. People voted against them because they could not hear their own voices in them. The statements themselves were not flawed, but the process for creating the statements was flawed.

I learned a valuable lesson through that experience: unless people can see themselves or hear their voice in the guiding statements, they will not buy into supporting and enacting them. There must be ample opportunities for people to share their voice throughout the process so that when the final statements are produced, people will feel a sense of personal connection to what has been created.

Our system for generating new guiding statements involves four congregational gatherings before the statements are presented for approval:

1. A history gathering

2. A scriptural gathering

3. An experiential gathering

4. A first draft gathering

I always recommend that the gatherings be accompanied by a meal. It doesn't matter whether they occur on a weekday evening, a Saturday morning, or following worship on Sunday. In all cases, a good meal (please, don't cut costs by just serving snacks) should be served so that participants can sit at tables together and engage in conversation. Relationships are absolutely crucial to organizational development, as people tend to go with their friends. Each gathering should be publicized for several weeks prior so that everyone in the congregation is made aware that it will be happening. It's important not to give anyone an excuse for not participating. No one should be able to say later, "No one told me that this was happening." I recommend using several forms of communication—mail, email, the website, newsletters, bulletins, and announcements in worship—to draw people's attention to the gatherings.

It's helpful, although not totally necessary, for the vision team to set the dates for all the upcoming gatherings at one time so that they can all be publicized multiple times together. When doing this, be sure to spread the dates in a workable rhythm that doesn't make people feel like they are needing to attend too often, while also keeping the events close enough to be perceived as being part of the same process. Encourage people to attend and to spread the word and bring their friends. Again, people go with their friends. If they know that friends will be there to support them and engage with them in the conversation, they will be more likely to attend. If your congregation has small groups, use the small group leaders in encouraging participation.

The History Gathering

I prefer that the history gathering be the first event to engage the congregation in conversation. Prior to this gathering, the vision team should create a large time line that can be placed on the wall in the space where the gathering is to occur. The time line needs to be large enough so that people can see it from the tables and provide enough space so people can add items or details to the time line. The time line should cover the congregation's entire existence, from inception to current date, highlighting significant events in the life of the congregation. This list should include building projects, significant community occurrences such as natural disasters or catastrophes, and key ministry events that people remember. I also like for the time line to mark the dates of pastoral terms (beginning and end), along with vital data (especially membership and worship attendance). The onset or elimination of debt is also a helpful item to be included on the time line, as this can be a relevant factor in congregational growth or decline. It's not helpful to list the vital data annually, but depending on the age of the congregation, showing the vital data in consistent intervals, such as every ten to twenty years, can help people to identify trends. For congregations that are quite old (the congregation where I was raised was founded in 1854), there is no need to stretch the time line all the way back to the beginning. As a guide for older congregations, I typically recommend that the time line start with the year that the longest-tenured member either joined or was born.

While conducting a history gathering with a congregation in Rapid City, South Dakota, one of the items that was included on the time line was the great Rapid City flood of 1972. As the facilitator for the conversation, I knew nothing about the Rapid City flood and began to ask the participants how the flood affected both the city and the congregation. What I learned was astonishing. The flood claimed the lives of 238 people, a record for the Rapid City community, and the funeral homes were overtaxed in dealing with all the deceased. One of the leading funeral directors in town was a member of the congregation and asked for help from the people of the church to transport bodies and conduct funerals. The church rallied to help the funeral director, resulting in most of the funerals being held at the church. The congregation viewed this as a positive moment in their history, an experience where they felt great satisfaction in being able to serve their community in the midst of such a catastrophic time. Examples such as this are invaluable as we begin the identity and purpose conversation for the congregation within their particular context. These stories help people to grasp ways in which the church can participate in transforming the culture of the greater community through acts of service and generosity.

During the meal, people are invited to add to the time line other significant dates. People might add dates of youth gatherings, retreats, or other ministries that played a key role in their personal spiritual development. Some will include dates of baptisms, confirmations, weddings, or funerals. Remember, it's important that people see their stories within the congregational story so they can make an emotional connection with the life of the congregation.

Following the meal, and after everyone has had a chance to add their information to the time line, the facilitator (who could be the pastor or a member of the vision team but needs to be someone good at helping people to tell their stories) will begin to walk the participants through the time line, starting at the beginning. The facilitator does not need to read every detail on the time line but is charged with drawing attention to key items, paying particular attention to trends. Instead of the facilitator giving explanations for the trends, the facilitator should engage the participants to assess and give voice to their perception of trends.

For example, when noticing a steady decline in attendance or membership, the facilitator could ask, "What was happening here that led to such a trend?" Participants are then free to talk about such things as growth or decline in the community, conflict that split the congregation, dynamic pastoral leadership (or the opposite). It's important that the facilitator help people to recognize that this is not a time of judgment, but simply a time to tell the congregation's story in order to build on past successes while learning from past failures. A phrase that I like to use when working with congregations is that we are called to "fail forward." Failure isn't a sin. It's a reality of life. If we never fail, we're never trying. The question is, What can we learn from our failures so that we can try more wisely in the future?

If the facilitator sees an added item that is intriguing (for instance, someone once wrote, "I was found by Christ"), the facilitator might want to ask, "Who wrote this item?" and invite the person to tell a bit of his or her story. These individual stories can be extraordinarily powerful as they engage emotion and demonstrate at a deep level the personal impact of the congregation. The facilitator should give people permission to speak freely when a historical item is addressed so that they can add detail to the event. The facilitator is charged with not allowing any single person(s) to filibuster the conversation and to keep the dialogue flowing smoothly. These gatherings, including both meal and conversation, should take no more than two hours. If the gatherings go too long, it will deter people from attending future gatherings. Before dismissing the gathered, the facilitator should thank everyone for their participation and provide the date for the next gathering along with a brief description of its focus, while encouraging everyone to attend and bring friends. The facilitator may also encourage the participants to talk to others about this gathering to help spread the word about the visioning process.

After the event, members of the vision team should collect the time line to gather information from it that will be used during the creation of the guiding statements. The team should pay close attention to the trends of growth and decline to identify the factors that played a key role in the congregation's progress. For example, when the congregation was very engaged in the local community, the congregation grew. When conflict occurred, the congregation declined and has never recovered. This information will be particularly helpful in the generation of core values that can direct the congregation toward a more inclusive, outward focus, while also providing values that aid in addressing conflict or differing viewpoints. A couple of vision team members should be tasked with gleaning such information from the time line and presenting it at the next team meeting.

Recently, as we've been replicating this process throughout the ELCA, I've received feedback from some colleagues who have gotten pushback from their leaders over conducting the history gathering. Their reasoning was multifaceted. It turns out that some struggling congregations feel they have conducted such retrospectives multiple times over the years as they've engaged with consultants regarding missional development. Not replicating this process is fine as long as (1) the process was conducted within the past three years, (2) it was open for all congregants to participate, and (3) they still have the notes from the conversation. If any of these three items is missing, then I strongly encourage conducting another history gathering.

Other colleagues reported that their leaders were reticent about conducting a history gathering because the congregation had experienced very divisive conflict that resulted in a congregational split, and they did not want to rehash the details and potentially do further harm. While I understand the pain of congregational conflict intimately, conducting the history gathering will prove to be more fruitful than harmful. A skilled facilitator can help the participants to navigate through the period of conflict without drawing blame or judgment. It also provides an opportunity for people to voice the pain that they experienced and may continue to experience because of the conflict. The facilitator can draw on a hopeful message that, despite the conflict, the congregation is still there, and God is not done with them yet. Every history gathering of which I have been a part has resulted in deep emotional sharing that leads to a sense of hopeful anticipation for the next chapter in the life of the congregation.

The Scriptural Gathering

It would be foolish and unwise to create guiding statements that are not firmly based in Scripture. However, how do you choose which scriptural verses will be the foundation for your new document? The scriptural gathering is intended to give people voice regarding passages in the Bible with which they have a deep personal connection. As this gathering is publicized, nature of the gathering should be described, and people should be encouraged to think about what passages are important to them. Be sure to let people know that they don't have to know the Bible well or even be able to identify the chapter and verse of the passages. The pastor and others will be on hand at the gathering to help them find and identify their favorite Bible verses. The invention of smartphones has helped greatly in expediting this process. When I facilitate such gatherings, I walk from table to table with my web browser on Bible Gateway. When someone asks me, "Pastor, where's that verse about 'rejoice always'?" if I can't cite it by memory, I can do a quick search on my phone to find it.

Be sure that each table has several Bibles, along with stacks of sticky notes and pens. Following the meal, the facilitator invites the participants to put one Bible verse on each single sticky note along with a brief explanation for why they feel a connection to that passage. It's important that each sticky note only have one verse, because the vision team will sort the sticky notes into categories as they process the information. For instance, I might write: "Psalm 23—It was my grandmother's favorite passage. I think of her every time I hear it." The participants only need to list the book, chapter, and verse on the sticky note. It's not necessary to write out the entire passage. However, the explanation for why they feel a connection is critically important, because that gives insight into the values behind the

Scripture selection. Also, please discourage people from putting their names on their sticky notes, because this helps to remove bias as the vision team processes the information.

Using my note above about Psalm 23, the vision team could conclude the value of family and relationships is a key factor in why that passage was chosen. As they identify passages, participants are encouraged to share with their table mates what they're writing on the sticky notes and to help each other. Some will feel like they don't know the Bible well enough but still want to participate. Hearing others' stories will help to trigger thoughts and ideas in those who feel ill-equipped. It's important that every participant identify at least one passage with which they feel a connection.

I gain great joy from circulating from table to table when facilitating a scriptural gathering. I especially like asking, "What about this passage is important for you?" From that simple question you can begin to learn about a person's theology and life story as they share why a particular verse about love or forgiveness speaks to them. The goal is to get all the tables engaging in conversations at this level so that people will hear one another's voices as a way of demonstrating the diversity within the congregation while also keeping the focus on life experience. One story always triggers another story. One passage always hints toward another passage. The facilitator and the pastor(s), along with a couple members of the vision team, can help fuel such conversations by simply asking open-ended questions that get people talking.

A story that stands out in my memory occurred while facilitating a scriptural gathering in a congregation in Colorado. The people at one of the tables were working silently, each scanning the Bible and occasionally writing down a verse. I happened to look at one note written by a man that simply said, "Matthew

18—Forgiveness." Fully aware of the content of Matthew 18, I asked him, "Why is Matthew 18 so important to you?" He looked up from his writing and without glancing at the others said boldly, "I'm a recovering alcoholic. I know firsthand what it means to need forgiveness seventy times seven." Wow! I was struck by the depth of his vulnerability. Another woman at the table chimed in, "I'm also in recovery. I've been sober almost twenty-five years." Suddenly, the conversation among this group reached far greater depths than simply discussing Scripture verses. Everyone became engaged in a dialogue about how we all need grace, love, and forgiveness as we go through life.

When the facilitator notices that the activity at the tables is ceasing, then he or she gets the attention of the participants and invites them to share one or two of the passages they've chosen and the reasoning for why they chose them. If someone says, "I chose Psalm 23," the facilitator might also ask the large group, "Did anyone else choose Psalm 23?" This sort of engagement serves to create connection and energy among the participants. Even if someone is the only one to choose a certain passage, it provides the large group insight and perspective into the diversity of thoughts and feelings contained within the congregation. This will help people to accept the guiding statements, even if they see words or phrases that don't necessarily speak to them, remembering that others think and feel differently than they do. Hopefully, everyone will ultimately experience connections with certain statements while giving grace and space for the parts of the statements that don't reflect their own viewpoints. Before dismissing everyone, the facilitator thanks the people for their participation, provides the date for the next gathering along with a brief description of its purpose, and encourages everyone to attend and bring friends.

At the end of the scriptural gathering, a couple of vision team members are tasked with gathering all the sticky notes and collating them based on the verses and the values reflected in the comments. For instance, we would anticipate that several sticky notes would say "John 3:16"; therefore, all that have this verse on them would form one pile. However, people may have different reasons for choosing this passage, and thus on a notepad or whiteboard, a list of separate values will need to be created. As an example, one person listing John 3:16 might focus on "God's love," while another person might focus on "faith." These values would be listed separately in the notes, even though both are tied to the same Scripture verse. The stacks of sticky notes along with the list of values is then brought to the next vision team meeting for conversation and processing.

The Experiential Gathering

The third gathering, which I call the experiential gathering, is intended to encourage people to reflect on the positive impact that the church (not necessarily the current congregation) has had on their lives. The reason we do not restrict the experiences to the current congregation is that we are trying to create a focus on the role of church, in general, for transforming lives. We want people to begin to think about how the church has shaped their identity, purpose, and outlook on life as children, youth, or adults. That's also the reason we stress only positive experiences. This is not the forum for complaining about or criticizing the church. The history gathering is the forum where past conflicts can be discussed from the perspective of gaining positive insights from which the congregation can evolve. At the experiential gathering, we're attempting to draw people into conversations regarding why the church matters and why the participants choose to continue to be involved. Like the scriptural gathering, participants should be told in advance about the intent of this gathering so that people have time to prepare their reflections and don't feel put on the spot.

Again, sticky notes and pens are placed on all the tables. Following the meal, the facilitator invites people to think about how the church has positively affected them. They are encouraged to identify key events in the church that were particularly meaningful. For example, some might write about their baptisms or their children's baptisms. Someone might recall a time of difficulty or pain when the congregation supported them with visits, prayers, and meals. There are no right or wrong responses to the inquiry. The intent is to glean from the participants why church is important to them.

Participants are encouraged to write one experience per sticky note along with a short description of why this event was particularly meaningful. For example, the person who writes about a time of need when the congregation was there for them might add, "It gave us strength and hope." Participants are encouraged to discuss their experiences with their table mates as story connects to story. One person's sharing might trigger a recollection in another person. Also, such stories often connect to the human psyche and emotions, which generate a deeper awareness for the value and importance of a faith community. Although some may have negative or bitter feelings toward the church, hearing stories of life, love, service, and generosity will help to assuage the negative.

An older woman at a church in Pennsylvania began to weep in her chair as she wrote, "The church saved my life." I noticed people gathering around her to comfort her, so I moved over near the table. I saw what she had written on the sticky note and asked, "Can you tell us about that?" She wiped her face and blew her nose and said,

I grew up in an extremely abusive home. It was horrible. My friend who lived down the street invited me one week to go with her to Sunday school and church. My family didn't attend church. I asked my parents for permission and was surprised when they agreed to let me go. That first Sunday, I didn't have very nice clothes to wear. Actually, I didn't know that you were even expected to get dressed up for church. But thankfully, my friend invited me for a sleepover the night before and when she saw that I didn't have church clothes, she let me wear some of hers. It was an incredible experience. Not only did I love everything about Sunday school and the worship service, I got a break from the insanity in my home. It became a weekly practice. I would go to my friend's house for dinner each Saturday, spend the night, go to church with her family the next morning, then return to my home after lunch. I'm convinced that that break every week is what gave me the strength to deal with all the abuse I experienced at home.

She started weeping again, "The church saved my life." My eyes filled with tears as I thought to myself, "The church saves lives. Thank God for that."

Once the facilitator assesses that people have begun to stop writing, the facilitator then engages in large-group conversation, inviting people to share one or two of their reflections. The purpose for this exercise is, again, to allow people to hear the different experiences that have occurred within the church that have been transformative and life giving. It helps to support the work that the vision team will do in producing the guiding statements as people begin to positively anticipate what is to be developed. Once the large-group conversation has ended, the facilitator thanks the participants and explains the process to follow. The vision team will now take all the collected data and information and begin to form new guiding statements for the congregation. Once they have a solid first draft, the team will convene a gathering (probably following worship on a Sunday) to reveal the statements to the congregation and garner feedback. The team will communicate that date once a first draft has been created.

Following the conclusion of the gathering, one or two vision team members are tasked with collecting all the sticky notes and then collating them to bring to the next vision team meeting. The sticky notes should be placed in piles of shared or common experiences (e.g., baptisms, weddings, funerals, care, community), and a separate list of values should be created based on the explanations for why these experiences mattered to people (e.g., hope, joy, strength, peace, love).

Step Five: Creating the Guiding Statements

The responsibility now lies with the vision team to sort through all the data and information that they've been collecting in order to create guiding statements, which consist of a vision, mission, core values, and tagline that will guide the congregation in their strategic and missional cultural development. It works best if the team has a room with a large whiteboard that they can use as they sort through the information. If a large whiteboard is not available, then large white Post-It Easel Pads with sheets of paper that stick to the wall is another option. The focus now is on key words or short phrases that have surfaced through the demographic work (e.g., poverty, despair, suicide, addiction, youth), at the history gathering (e.g., service, peace-making, passion), during the scriptural gathering (e.g., love, faith, hope, service, generosity), and during the experiential gathering (e.g., welcoming, support, strength, joy, transformation). Don't try to edit or arrange the words initially. Have someone at the board writing as the other team members call out words or phrases. This is a pure brainstorming, shotgun approach. There will most likely be thirty or more words or phrases on the board (see image below of terms created by one of our partner congregations).

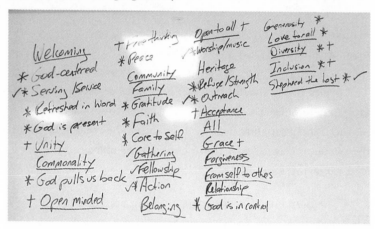

The next step is to begin to categorize the words and phrases into more generalized terms. I have found the best way to do this is to use symbols beside the words that indicate some form of commonality between particular terms. Notice in the image above that some words and phrases have more than one symbol beside them. Certain terms will often relate to a variety of categories. The group will need to discern in which category each term or phrase will ultimately land. The list of categories should be shorter than the initial list, but not sparse. We want to move slowly as we pare the terms and phrases down so that we do not overlook or omit an important and necessary concept from the guiding statements. The image below demonstrates the categories created from the initial list above.

Serve   Love   Community
Shepherd   All   God-centered
Inclusion   Outreach   Generosity
Diversity   Acceptance   Faith
Action   Unity   Gratitude
Open-minded   Fellowship   Free-thinking
Worship/music   Gathering   Grace

Once this categorical list has been generated, the vision team can begin to form the guiding statements. I've seen teams that choose to block a Saturday to go through this process up to creating the first draft of statements, while others choose to spread it over a couple weeks to give time for individual reflection between meetings. Either process will work. I recommend that the team begin with creating the core values. The values define the culture into which persons will be immersed. The strategic plan will also be generated from the core values (more on that to come). By beginning with the values, the vision team will create a snapshot for what the congregational culture will look like. Then, they are able to develop a mission statement for how those values will be lived out, followed by a vision statement for what the outcome is to be, and finally a tagline that will communicate to the greater community the identity and essence of the congregation. For instance, the guiding statements of Abiding Hope are as follows:

Core Values

Authentic worship

Intentional relationships

Sacrificial service

Radical generosity

Mission

Equip all to be the heart, hands, and feet of Jesus in the world

Vision

A wholly unleashed faith community

Tagline

Experience real life

The guiding statements, when read together, create a narrative flow:

> At Abiding Hope, we immerse people into *authentic worship, intentional relationships, sacrificial service, and radical generosity* to *equip all to be the heart, hands, and feet of Jesus in the world* to create a *wholly unleashed faith community* so that all may *experience real life.*

Beginning with the values, one statement flows out of and into the next to clearly define the culture we seek to generate.

I recommend three to five values so they can be easily memorized and used consistently throughout the life of the congregation. Notice that the Abiding Hope values each have two words. This was intentional in order to use eight words for our cultural foundation. At first glance, it appears that we have four values, and the focus is on the second term in each phrase (worship, relationships, service, and generosity). There's no question that these words receive the most attention throughout the life of the congregation. However, the modifying words that start each value hold great significance regarding the Abiding Hope way of life as we strive to be authentic, intentional, sacrificial, and radical in all that we do. Two-word value phrases are still easy to memorize, while increasing the clarity of the congregational culture that the vision team seeks to create.

Figure 3.3 demonstrates the process of the vision team of our partner congregation Rejoice Church as it moved from individual terms to statements. Notice the column of words on the left side of the image and at the top of the second column. These were phrases or statements they brainstormed from the list of words on the right, which reflected their own experience and expectation for the identity and purpose of the congregation. From that brainstorming list, the team then began to form the values and the mission. Initially, they had four two-word values but decided collectively that the phrase "unity in diversity" was not a value but more of an outcome they hoped to generate. The values were the practices that they would immerse people in to create a specified outcome that would ultimately include unity in diversity. Thus, they settled on three core val-

ues: passionate inclusion, grateful service, and generous community. They identified *passion, gratitude,* and *generosity* to be the
modifiers that would also play a key role in the congregational
culture they sought to create in addition to *inclusion, service,* and
community.

Tagline: Rejoice Church
Breathe New Life

Vision: Humanity Unleashed through love

Mission: Fortify all to live as children of God

Values: Passionate Inclusion
Grateful Service
Generous Community

Once the team identified the values, I then asked, "As we
immerse people into passionate inclusion, grateful service, and
generous community, what will we be 'doing'?" After some conversation, one person said, "People will be fortified to live as
children of God." Aha! We had our mission statement: "Fortify
all to live as children of God." I then asked, "If all are fortified
to live as children of God, what will be the outcome?" Again,

after some conversation, the team agreed that this is the process by which humanity would be unleashed through love. We then had a vision statement: "Humanity unleashed through love." Finally, I asked, "How do you communicate this to the greater community? What gift are you giving? What are you ultimately inviting people into?" After a bit more conversation and word-smithing, the team agreed that what people seek and yearn to be able to do is "breathe new life." That became the tagline.

And now they had a narrative flow of guiding statements that would define the culture of the congregation:

> At Rejoice Church, we immerse people into *passionate inclusion, grateful service, and generous community* to *fortify all to live as children of God,* which creates a *humanity unleashed through love* so that all may *breathe new life.*

It's important to recognize that this process took months as the data and information were collected. After the data were collated, the vision team held an all-day Saturday workday to begin crafting the statements. They did a great job in developing this first draft in about six hours. However, I was with them, helping them to sort through all the information and asking guiding questions that enabled them to move rather quickly. It would have been more difficult had they not had the benefit of my experience and guidance. Thus, I advocate for congregations that are not experienced in such matters to enlist the assistance of a partner congregation that can help guide them through the process.

Congregational Gathering to Unveil the First Draft of the Guiding Statements

Following the generation of the first draft of guiding statements, the vision team then schedules a time following worship on a Sunday morning to unveil their work to the congregation. Please note that this unveiling is not to create space for more wordsmithing by the congregation. That would be disastrous and a huge waste of time. This event is intended to get feedback that either affirms what the vision team has produced or calls for the vision team to return to the drawing board. The primary questions to pose are, Can you see your voice in these statements? and, Would this be a culture in which you'd want to participate?

As with the other congregational gatherings, a meal should be served to gather people around tables to create a sense of community. I far prefer to have people at tables together rather than sitting in chairs or pews as if attending a lecture. At one such meeting, the vision team had created large boards containing the guiding statements that could be placed on easels and easily read from afar. It's important that the statements be veiled so that no one can see them during the meal. Following the meal, it's best for the chair of the team to greet and thank everyone for coming. This person should also call on the pastor to pray. Following the prayer, the chairperson explains the vision team process for how demographic data were collected and information was gathered from the congregation. The chair describes the process for how the vision team sorted through the information and generated the statements.

The chairperson should also ask whether anyone has any questions regarding the process. After all questions are addressed, the chairperson unveils the core values and describes a bit about their meaning. The chairperson can then ask for questions or comments regarding the core values. The chairperson may want to explain to the gathered group that this is not the time for corporate wordsmithing. This is a time for people to provide feedback as to whether they identify their voice in the statements and feel that the statements are clear in reflecting the congregational culture they seek to create.

After conversation regarding the values wanes, the chairperson unveils the mission statement, vision statement, and tagline one at a time in order to address each individually. Once all the statements have been unveiled and discussed, the chairperson reads the narrative flow of the statements to define the culture that will be created. No vote should be taken at this time, but the chairperson should ask whether the congregation feels the vision team has done their work or whether more work needs to be done. If the consensus is positive, then the vision team will take the guiding statements to the council for approval. If the council approves the statements, then the council will call for a congregational gathering to formally adopt the new guiding statements. Once the guiding statements are approved by the congregation, the vision team is thanked for their work and disbanded. At this point, the pastor and others will begin the work of creating a strategic plan built from the core values. Since many pastors lack experience and find building a strategic plan to be a daunting task, the anchor church model can provide the necessary support and coaching for this process. Chapter 5 will address the anchor church model and process.

4

STRATEGIC CULTURAL DEVELOPMENT

Simplicity is the ultimate sophistication.

—Leonardo Da Vinci

I have found through working with several congregations and pastors in recent years that generating clear strategic cultural development is an incredibly difficult and daunting task. First of all, few pastors have much experience, if any at all, in creating a strategic focus for the congregation. Second, it feels big and unwieldy to begin thinking through how to take the concepts of the new culture and make them actionable. Finally, it's not a quick process. It takes time to create an initial draft, to engage other leaders to understand their goals and expectations, to discern how best to phase in the strategic plan, as not all things

can be completed at once, and then to align the system to function at its highest capacity. This is the point in the process of
congregational development where most pastors get stuck and/
or require assistance. Certainly, within the ELCA, each synod's
director for evangelical mission is trained in developing strategic plans, but it's not possible for one person to accompany
every pastor within the synod who needs support. Before we
begin to define the process for generating an effective strategic
plan, we need to explore the concept of organizational intelligence so that we do not create a strategy whose aims are developmental dead ends.

Organizational Intelligence

The author and leader on whom I rely most for guidance in
organizational intelligence is Russ Crabtree.[1] Crabtree has studied national denominations, judicatories, congregations, pastors, and congregational members to assess how some
congregations are vitalized and healthy while others struggle
to stay alive. Crabtree's work does not focus so much on the
quantitative data of membership, attendance, and giving, since
that information is easy to access. Instead, Crabtree has sought
to identify congregational members' perceptions, experiences,
and aspirations for their congregation, because this information
speaks better to the vitality of a congregation. According to
Crabtree's assessment, only about 10 percent of ELCA congregations are what he would categorize as "transformational or
vitalized." I would imagine the same to be true for most mainline
denominations within the United States.

It's also worth noting that most pastors are not familiar with
the concepts of organizational intelligence and are certainly are
not experienced in it. To my knowledge, it is not yet an area of

1. For a list of Russ Crabtree's books, see chap. 3, n. 1, 84.

focus in seminary training, unless we consider the contextual part of the seminary education in which some pastoral interns might be assigned to organizationally intelligent supervisors. However, we currently have no way of measuring how many students have such experiences. Personally, I'd like to see denominations require training in organizational intelligence as an intentional part of both theological and contextual education for seminarians.

If vitality is about a congregation's ability for agency, that is, to be strong and active, it stands to reason that our first foray into assessing a congregation's culture is to measure the satisfaction and energy of the congregation.[2] Satisfaction is not to be understood as whether congregants like or are happy with their congregation. Satisfaction represents congregants self-reporting that participation within the congregation generates a sense of *wholeness* within congregants. This notion relates to the concept that congregational focus should be placed on people, not programs. Recall that we've defined salvation as drawing people into oneness with God, other, and creation, which is a restorative process generating wholeness, wellness, and healing for both the individual and the cosmos. Crabtree's research seeks to identify how effective a congregation might be in this regard by assessing the perceptions and experiences of the congregants. His research indicates that congregations that do this well have a higher level of vitality than congregations that don't.

The other side of the satisfaction coin is what Crabtree calls energy. The energy of the congregation is its ability to clearly articulate its missional focus and direction. Crabtree explains,

In its Latin and Greek roots, energy is nuanced in the direction of "work" or "force of engagement." This is the way we are using the word when we talk about congregational health and vitality.

2. Crabtree, *State of the Evangelical Lutheran Church*, 21–30.

A high-energy congregation is one where members experience a compelling purpose or message combined with a high level of engagement, in contrast to a congregation where members are simply watching others or going through the motions of religious activity.[3]

When we multiply satisfaction with energy within a congregation, we find that the congregation has an increased opportunity toward vitality (satisfaction × energy = vitality). Crabtree would call this a "promising pathway" toward vitality.

Conversely, Crabtree's research has demonstrated that simply being Lutheran or Presbyterian or Episcopalian is not a key factor in congregational vitality. Congregations that choose to make denominational identity their primary means for attracting new people to the congregation will fail. About five years ago, we chose to take "Lutheran" off our sign, website, and other materials and simply become "Abiding Hope Church." The reasons we gave at the time were as follows:

1. Martin Luther said, "Do not call yourselves Lutheran. You are Christians. Identify with Christ, not me." Many Lutheran congregations in Europe are simply called "Evangelical."

2. Denominational loyalty is dead. Very few people were coming to Abiding Hope because we're Lutheran.

3. For more than ten years, many new congregations of the ELCA stopped including "Lutheran" in their names.

4. We are included as Lutheran in the media of the ELCA and the Rocky Mountain Synod, along with all the online search engines, so that people who do want

3. Crabtree, *State of the Evangelical Lutheran Church*, 22.

to find an ELCA congregation in Littleton, Colorado, will still be able to find us.

The results of removing "Lutheran" from our sign and website were immediate and nothing short of astounding. We began to experience more guests in worship who would ask us, "What kind of church is this?" When we'd tell them "Lutheran," they were shocked and would say things like, "My grandmother is Lutheran, and her congregation is nothing like this," or, "I grew up Lutheran and thought that church was boring and old-fashioned." What happened was that the people who were church shopping at the large, nondenominational community churches began to check out Abiding Hope as well. Unbeknownst to us, having "Lutheran" on the sign and website served as a deterrent because many people either perceived Lutheran churches to be old-fashioned, boring, and institutional, or something that they aren't, and thus they never even gave us a look. We have found that many people have roots in the mainline denominations and enjoy liturgy, but only when it's combined with good music and preaching and encapsulated in a community of high satisfaction and energy.

Crabtree's research also found that congregations of high satisfaction and energy tend to have more of an external versus internal focus. In fact, participants within congregations that are inwardly focused report significantly less satisfaction than participants in outwardly focused congregations. This doesn't mean that an externally focused congregation neglects its members, simply that the congregation recognizes that the path to wholeness doesn't come through catering to one's own needs but in pouring oneself out (*ekstasis*) in service and generosity toward others. Such a culture is more about way of life than it is about programmatic development. It's about being more than doing. As we further explore strategic cultural development, we must keep a clear focus on this idea so that we do not simply retreat into creating new programs. Into what culture are we inviting people? How are people experiencing wholeness through their participation within the congregational culture? Can people clearly identify what it looks like to live the congregation's values at home, work, school, neighborhood, and beyond?

In addition to external focus, Crabtree found that congregations that demonstrate healthy hospitality with guests and members tend to experience greater vitality than congregations that merely seek to disseminate information. At first, this seems like a rather simple distinction, but on deeper exploration, we find that most congregations prefer to disseminate information rather than engage in true hospitality. The fundamental difference between the two is that hospitality is relational, while information is not.

Imagine that some guests come to your house for a gathering. Some have never been there before, while others have been there many times. You're probably not going to hand out a flier that demonstrates where the bathrooms are or to describe the sorts of wine you're serving. On the contrary, you will greet people as they arrive with a warm handshake or hug. You'll take their coat, tell them how glad you are to see them, walk them into the gathering to introduce them to others, show them where the bathrooms are, point out the food and drink, and ask whether they need anything. That's hospitality. Don't think that hospitality begins only when people arrive. On the contrary, hospitality began when you issued the invitation for people to come to your gathering. You either called them, sent them a personal note, or mentioned something to them when you saw them. The invitation itself was highly personal and relational. You didn't just post a flier on a random message board or place generic fliers on doors. You personally contacted the invitees to let them know that they mattered and that you desired for them to attend your event. That's hospitality.

Too often, congregations rely on disseminating information to try to draw new people to their congregation or to get members to show up at events. Even at Abiding Hope, people will contact the church office or walk up to one of the pastors before worship to ask, "Can you please announce this event or activity?" We always respond by saying, "No, we can't do that. But what you can do is reach out to your circles of relationship to invite people to attend." Sometimes people are offended if we will not announce their particular event. We do our best to explain why this isn't prudent and why we can't do it.

The reality is that very few people attend events because they read about it or heard an announcement during worship. The announcements are intended to fuel and support the key missional activities of the congregation, not every single activity taking place. After all, people tend to go with their friends. Time is the number-one commodity for people in our context, which means that for everything someone says yes to doing or attending, they've said no to five or six other things. Therefore, the best way to get participation is for friends to appeal to friends, or in other words, relational hospitality. Congregations that combine an external focus with healthy hospitality tend to experience greater vitality than congregations that are internally focused and information driven (external × hospitality = vitality).

Another promising pathway toward vitality, according to Crabtree's research, is what he calls *adaptable*, culture shifting, or missional flexibility. He explains,

> A lack of flexibility is often the underlying cause of many different problems that tend to occur over and over again. . . . Developing a

flexible culture is critical to church health and growth. Three elements are key to making that shift. First there must be a distinction between mission and programs. . . . Second, flexibility is learned by *doing* not by *thinking*. . . . Finally, developing flexibility, like any culture change, requires leadership with a particularly heavy dose of courage. Even the most well-managed change process will elicit a level of dissatisfaction.[4]

Change is difficult. Cultural architecture requires a certain level of high pain or frustration tolerance. There also needs to be a willingness to take risks, with the expectation that failure will bring knowledge and experience that can be applied toward more positive results. Leaders who have a high need to please or appease everyone will struggle with creating a culture of flexibility, because they will tend to back down whenever people react negatively to the change. If you are someone who struggles in this regard, you would benefit from finding a mentor who is a demonstrated cultural architect and can accompany you through the storms of transition into transformation. A gifted mentor can help you to assess the turbulence and to understand it as an aspect of transition. Hopefully, then, you won't take negativity or pushback personally and will be equipped to lead the congregation consistently through the cultural transformation.

Adaptive Leadership

Adaptability does not mean that a congregation chooses to transform Sunday school into Bible Explorers. That's simply a programmatic or technical shift, not a cultural or adaptive shift. The preeminent leader in articulating adaptive versus technical shift is Ron Heifetz, the founder of the Center for Public Leadership at the Harvard Kennedy School. Heifetz's books are

4. Crabtree, *Penguins in the Pews*, 60–64.

incredible resources for aiding leaders in differentiating between moves and decisions that lead to lasting cultural transformation versus what Heifetz calls "technical shifts," which keep the culture the same and do not produce lasting change.[5] Heifetz explains,

> Adaptive leadership is an approach to making progress on the most important challenges you face in your piece of the world, presumably in your professional life but perhaps in your personal life as well. Our concepts, tools, and tactics aim to help mobilize people toward some collective purpose, a purpose that exists beyond your own individual ambition.[6]

For Heifetz, the term *adaptive* does not just mean that the leader adapts (although we will demonstrate that adaptive leaders must be aware of their attitudes and behaviors, because these can derail the transformation process). On the contrary, it means that leaders envision and generate a culture that serves to transform and mobilize those within the culture to live and perform in ways that generate positive results, not only for individuals but for the organization as a whole. Heifetz makes the point that transforming a culture to create adaptive change within an organization is incredibly hard work. If it were easy, anyone and everyone would be doing it. (Recall that Crabtree estimates that only about 10 percent of ELCA congregations are transformed and vitalized.) Generating clarity of vision and strategic planning is part of what leads to adaptive shift. The other and arguably more difficult part is the role of the very disciplined,

---

5. Ron Heifetz's well-known books on adaptive leadership are *Leadership without Easy Answers* (Cambridge, MA: Harvard University Press, 2018); *Leadership on the Line: Staying Alive through the Dangers of Change* (Cambridge, MA: Harvard Business Review Press, 2017); *The Practice of Adaptive Leadership: Tools and Tactics for Changing Your Organization and the World* (Cambridge, MA: Harvard Business Review Press, 2009).

6. Heifetz, *Practice of Adaptive Leadership*, 3.

consistent, self-aware, and culturally aware leader who steadily enacts and drives forward the adaptive shift. Heifetz says,

> The practice of leadership, like the practice of medicine, involves two core processes: diagnosis first and then action. And these two processes unfold in two dimensions: toward the organization or social system you are operating in and toward yourself. That is, you diagnose what is happening in your organization or community and take action to address the problems you have identified. But to lead effectively, you also have to examine and take action toward yourself in the context of the challenge. In the midst of action, you have to be able to reflect on your own attitudes and behavior to better calibrate your interventions into the complex dynamics of organizations and communities. You need perspective on yourself as well as on the systemic context in which you operate.[7]

In my experience, many pastors who can vision and plan fail at the execution aspect of adaptive change because they find it difficult to handle the situation when parishioners cry out in pain and blame the pastor for their discomfort. It's one thing to be leading adaptive change in a business when all involved are paid employees who are required to follow the boss's instruction, get in line, and participate accordingly. It's an entirely different animal to lead adaptive change in a congregation full of unpaid members who come to church voluntarily. When the membership, or at least a critical mass of the membership, begins to cry out because they aren't comfortable with the new culture, and they point to the pastor as the source of their pain, it's not uncommon for the pastor and key leaders to feel coerced to stop the adaptive shift and return to the old, failing culture.

I have witnessed countless examples of pastors and leaders

7. Heifetz, *Practice of Adaptive Leadership*, 6.

who begin the adaptive process only to stop midstream and return to the old. The result is often disastrous, as many people leave the congregation during the turbulence, while the pastor and leaders lose all leadership capital and credibility, thus disabling them from engaging in the adaptive change process again. It's extraordinarily difficult, if not impossible, for the same pastor and leaders to reignite a new adaptive shift within the same congregation where they already backed down due to emotional pressure. Congregational leadership can be similar to parenting. (I'm not labeling parishioners as children; I'm simply pointing out the similar dynamic between congregational leadership and parenting.) When a parent reverses a decision (often a no) because of heavy emotional coercion (e.g., crying and begging) from the child, the child learns that he can manipulate that parent by whining and complaining. The adaptive leader of a congregation, just like a parent, needs to be courageous and consistent in their approach, or a toxic culture of manipulation and coercion will emerge.

This is one of the very reasons why I am advocating for struggling congregations to be accompanied by vitalized congregations toward the process of strategic cultural development. It is incredibly hard work to remain focused and consistent when a congregation begins to undergo turbulence. Two parents have a far easier time dealing with emotional manipulation from their child than a single parent.

Recall the story in chapter 2 in which Pastor Joel was confronted during worship by Stella. This wasn't the first time that Stella had behaved this way. She had pulled these sorts of manipulative ploys with several of the previous pastors, yet no one was able to address her in a manner that would not only put an end to the toxicity but also invite her into healthy participation within the life of the congregation. Pastor Joel was able to accomplish this seemingly impossible task because he had the accompanying support of a seasoned mentoring pastor and healthy leaders. Without such support, these situations often result in the pastor backing down and cowering to the manipulation and control of the parishioner. This either greatly hinders the pastor's ability to generate adaptive change, or the pastor and the parishioner end up in a standoff that tends to split the congregation. Neither path ever leads to health and vitality. Ever!

Under strong, healthy, adaptive leadership, congregational conflict can be an enormous blessing that can serve to advance the generation of the new culture, just as the story of Pastor Joel and Stella demonstrated. Because of Joel's handling of the situation, his leadership capital and credibility shot through the roof within the congregation. This enabled him to continue to move the congregation toward the envisioned new culture. Conflict is neither good nor bad. How we choose to handle conflict is where the value lies. The healthy adaptive leader addresses conflict through the defined values, mission, and vision of the organization, pointing all toward the desired culture and identifying attitudes and behaviors that do not reflect or have become an obstacle to the newly developing culture.

However, it's not always congregants that derail the adaptive shift of the congregation. Sometimes it's the pastor's attitudes and behaviors that get in the way of the development.

Back in the mid-1990s I attended an Alban Institute workshop addressing the four models of congregation based on worship attendance. One key point that stuck with me concerned the attitudes and behaviors of the pastor that were necessary to transition from a congregation that worshipped in the range of 50 to 150 people to 151 to 350. The instructor told us that a key reason why congregations don't evolve beyond about 175 average worship attendance is that the pastor has a high need to be in personal relationship with every member, and it's impossible for a pastor to be in direct relationship with more than about 150 parishioners at a time. As a congregation grows and more people join, some members might complain that they "don't get to see enough of the pastor anymore," or "he spends most of his attention on the new people." A pastor with a high need to relate to all will stop spending time working to grow the congregation so that she can spend more time with the current parishioners.

I posit that the pastors who tend to struggle the most with adaptive shift in congregations are pastors who score high on mercy as a spiritual gift. In my experience, persons with a high mercy gift struggle more than most with making tough decisions that might result in someone becoming upset. Such leaders feel a strong tug not to do anything that might cause discomfort. They might also reverse a decision because it appeared to cause discomfort. There are countless scriptural examples of adaptive leadership in which a leader is tempted to reverse course due to the cries of others, but then makes a conscious decision to go forward toward the original aim for the sake of the community and culture.

Consider the story of Moses leading the people out of slavery in Egypt toward the land promised through the Abrahamic covenant. These texts even have a not-so-flattering name, the murmuring tradition, when the Israelites convinced themselves that they were better off under the enslavement of the Egyptians than as free people moving toward the promised land. Moses goes up on the mountain, according to Numbers 11:11–15, to tell God that he can no longer handle the cries and complaints of the people and prefers that God "put me to death at once" (Num 11:15). Instead, God raises up seventy elders to assist Moses in leading the Israelites, and Moses continues to guide them toward Canaan. Had Moses died or chosen to lead the people back to Egypt, they all would have been destroyed.

The other story of adaptive leadership involves Jesus in Mark 8:31–33. Here Jesus explains to his disciples that they will be going to Jerusalem, where he will be rejected by the temple leaders, put to death, and then raised after three days. Peter admonishes Jesus. Instead of heeding Peter's emotional plea not to go to Jerusalem, Jesus rebukes Peter, saying, "Get behind me, Satan!" In this moment, Jesus's adaptive leadership is in question because of Peter's anxiety regarding what is to transpire.

The adaptive leader within the congregation must maintain a clear focus on the culture being generated in order to keep all in the organization properly aligned in that direction. If someone or something gets out of alignment or attempts to derail the cultural transformation, it's the responsibility of the adaptive leader to address the issue through the lens of the newly developing culture and to call all involved back into alignment. Doing this as a lone wolf is extraordinarily difficult, because such practices will engage every level of emotional intelligence, relational intelligence, and organizational intelligence within the leader. Further, the most toxic people in the room tend to be the noisiest. This often makes leaders question themselves and their leadership. It appears easier to give into the toxicity and to silence the cries, but such decisions are disastrous, as we've discussed, to both the organization and the future capabilities of the leader. Pushing forward toward the new cultural development, no matter how difficult it might appear, is the only path to lasting health and vitality.

Creating the Strategic Plan

The model of strategic plan that I have found to be most effective is one built from the core values of the congregation. To help demonstrate what such a plan looks like, I'm going to use the core values of Abiding Hope and show how our strategic development is constructed from them. Recall that the values are authentic worship, intentional relationships, sacrificial service, and radical generosity. The culture we seek to create needs to integrate all of these values into everything we do. In other words, we don't have aspects of our culture that focus on a single value at a time. Everything, and I mean *everything*, must include all four values to be part of the Abiding Hope culture. This means that small groups must integrate worship, relationships, service, and generosity. Outreach must integrate worship, relationships, service, and generosity. Even our worship life must integrate all four values to be considered a legitimate part of the Abiding Hope culture. The best way to illustrate this is through a multidimensional matrix (see table below). Along the top of the matrix are the core values, while down the left side are particular ministries or areas of focus within the life of the congregation.

	Worship	Relationship	Service	Generosity
Worship Life				
Small Groups				
Outreach				
Spiritual Formation				

Each ministry (the left column of the matrix) has a leader, whether paid staff or unpaid congregant, who bears the responsibility for assuring that the culture of the team aligns with the culture of the congregation. Also, each aspect of the culture has a leader, whether paid staff or congregant, who is responsible for championing that aspect of the culture.

Consider the small group ministry as an example. The leader

of small groups is responsible for creating a leadership team that visions and plans how best to grow and develop small groups through identifying new small group leaders, helping people to get connected into groups, providing curricula and other resources for the groups, and assessing the progress of the ministry. Meanwhile, the person responsible for championing the core value of worship within the congregation serves as a resource to the leaders of small groups to ensure that the groups are immersed into the worship life of the congregation. For instance, small groups can be enlisted periodically to serve as ushers, greeters, worship assistants, and communion assistants, or to provide hospitality during worship services. Songs, sermons, liturgies, and prayers are provided online so that small groups can access and use them during their gathering times. The small group curriculum aligns with the current worship theme so that small group discussions become an extension of the worship life.

The same would hold true for integrating the other core values into small group activities. Certainly, forming relationships is integral to the process and functioning of small groups, and the person responsible for that core value would create resources that aid participants in going deeper with one another. The person responsible for service would provide ideas for how groups can engage in service opportunities together as well as encourage participants to serve at home, work, school, neighborhood, and beyond. Finally, the generosity leader would have small groups engage them in dialogue regarding being generous with their time, resources, forgiveness, compassion, and love within the congregation and in every aspect of their lives.

The matrix demonstrates how the culture within the congregation is to function, but the goal is for the congregational culture to spill over into the greater community through the lives of congregants. At Abiding Hope, we encourage our people to practice worship, relationships, service, and generosity in every aspect of their lives in order to draw their family members, coworkers, classmates, neighbors, and friends into the culture. One of the ways we encourage this is by equipping our members annually to conduct a "Neighbor Day" for the people on their street. This event is intended simply to gather neighbors together, to talk about life, and to be in relationship with one another. We tell our members not to talk about church but to use the time simply to connect. We also provide yard signs for our members prior to Christmas and Easter that offer an invitation to their neighbors to attend worship together. The goal is not to get everyone in the community to attend worship or become members of Abiding Hope. We believe that we can positively affect the culture of the community through our members living the congregational culture in every aspect of their lives.

The strategic plan is a living document intended to identify specific ways that we will work to generate the culture both within and beyond the doors of the congregation. Our process begins with identifying our key ministries: worship life, small groups, confirmation, spiritual development, new members, outreach, leadership development, children/youth/families, marketing and communication, resource development, and preschool/kindergarten. Each key ministry becomes a bulleted point so that underneath we can begin to identify our plan for integrating the core values into each ministry.

For example, under worship life we address how we will engage the worship planning process to generate seasonal themes that involve opportunities for contemplation and engagement within worship, as well as some level of takeaway that people can continue to practice throughout the week. We also plan for how best to connect people through hospitality, and we call people to engage in service and generosity. We create our own liturgies around the themes so that we can integrate the values into each worship experience beyond simply the sermon. The music and prayers also reflect the values and are presented differently according to each seasonal theme. For instance, in the fall, when we engage in our annual generosity appeal, the focus on generosity is more pronounced. However, even during that time, we continue to hold up the other values as well, as the culture depends on the integration of them all.

Once we have identified the key ministry areas and generated points under each for how we plan to integrate the values into each ministry, then we add a time line and metrics. It's important to recognize that we can't do everything at once. We need to space things out in a manageable pattern so that we do not overwhelm the congregation with too much transition too fast. We also need to think through a logical pattern for successive development. What is the foundation that needs to be laid before the first level can be constructed, which then leads to building levels two and three? In working with partner congregations going through holistic culture transformation, we typically create a three-phase, three-year plan. The first phase takes about six months and focuses on four key areas: worship, facility, leadership development, and fundraising.

The goal for addressing worship is not to transform it entirely but to begin to include the guiding statements in every aspect of worship life. As worship is our primary venue for immersion into the congregational culture, we want the vision, mission, core values, and tagline to appear in liturgies, prayers, children's messages, and sermons. We also want signs and banners around the worship space and other parts of the facility, bulletins, worship screens, and all other print materials to reflect the guiding statements.

A complete facility assessment needs to be conducted to determine whether any upgrades, additions, or modifications need to take place to serve the strategic development. Leaders must also be identified and equipped for the various teams and ministries included in the strategic plan. These leaders must become versed in the new culture and trained for how to immerse their team members into it. At Abiding Hope, we say that the first role of team leaders is to draw the members of their teams into worship, relationships, service, and generosity. The second role is to execute the responsibilities and tasks of the team. Cultural development precedes team execution. The other aspect of leadership development is assessing the staff structure and personnel. What staff roles will be necessary for living into the strategic plan? What particular gifts and skill sets will each staff person need to possess? Are current staff persons in the correct roles, and do they possess the needed gifts? What changes need to be made, and when?

Finally, some form of fundraising appeal needs to take place during phase 1 to generate the necessary funds needed to execute the strategic plan. (This includes staffing needs, facility needs, and ministry needs.) Hopefully, through the process of creating new guiding statements and the generation of the new strategic plan, the congregation is sensing forward movement and development, around which they are getting energized and excited. This is the perfect time to ask for people to step up in their generosity and invest in the new strategic cultural development of the congregation. (Surely generosity is mentioned somewhere in the new guiding statements, making this a wonderful opportunity to engage the congregation in conversation around this key value.)

As mentioned above, phase 1 lays the foundation for the following two phases and should be completed in about six months, and phase 2 should take about eighteen months, as it focuses on the creation and operation of the teams and ministries outlined within the strategic plan. This is the time when the congregation begins to experience forward movement into living out the new culture. This is the time of transition and change. This is also the time when conflict can occur, necessitating that leaders stand firm in the direction of strategic cultural development. To be clear, mistakes will be made. There will be aspects of the strategic plan that prove not to work or don't align or are too much too soon.

All of this is normal when engaging in the very difficult work of adaptive leadership. That's why the focus of phase 3, which is the final twelve months of the three-year strategic plan, is on assessing the progress of the cultural transformation. What's working? What's not working? What facility needs did we not anticipate? Do we have the financial fuel to accomplish our goals, or do we need to identify other funding sources? I'm often asked, "Does it really take a year to assess the progress? Can't that happen quicker?" Certainly, but remember, we're not just identifying the necessary course corrections, but we're making the necessary changes. For instance, if we identify that we don't have enough financial resources, the generosity team needs to go to work to create and execute a plan for generating more resources. If we encounter a facility need, the facility team needs to figure out how to address that need. Such things take time.

The other thing that begins in phase 3 is the pastor extending the strategic plan into the next year and beyond.[8] Recall that I mentioned above that the strategic plan is a living document.

---

8. I encourage one primary leader, usually the pastor, to take primary responsibility for building the strategic plan. However, this strategic plan is not done in a vacuum, without input from other key leaders.

This means that you don't start over each year in creating new strategic plans. You simply add on to the existing plan, making the necessary changes and continuing the strategic cultural development of the congregation.

Don't forget about the metrics either. This is a key point that many fail to include in their strategic planning or don't assess as they go forward. For example, if small group ministry is a key ministry for the congregation, how many small groups currently exist? In the next calendar year, how many total groups do you hope to have? How many people are currently engaged in the small group ministry? At the end of the next calendar year, how many people do you hope to have in small groups? The metrics help us to identify the tactics necessary to living into the strategic plan. For instance, the leader responsible for small groups knows that currently we have five groups. At this time next year, we'd like to have ten groups. The leader then knows that over the course of the year, she will need to raise up five new small group leaders and then help each of those leaders form new small groups. I have found that reporting on metrics monthly is too short of a time frame.

I have found that quarterly reporting of the metrics gives a developing snapshot for how things are progressing. Metrics are collected by assigned leaders, either paid staff or unpaid congregants, and reported to one person (this could be the pastor, pastor's assistant, or a top-tier leader), who collates the metrics and reports them to the leadership team. For example, if new small groups are not being developed after the first or second quarter, the leadership then must ask, "Why not?" It could be that the leader is struggling, or it could be a cultural dynamic. (For instance, we've found at Abiding Hope that it's easier to form small groups in the latter half of the year, because in the first part of the year people tend to be less willing to commit, as they are moving toward the end of the school year and toward vacation time.) As the leaders review the metrics, they need to assess and think through the information that the metrics are providing. If it's not the right season for developing a particular ministry, when is the right season, and what will be the tactical approach to achieving the goal?

In addition to quantitative metrics, it's important that the leaders find ways to create qualitative metrics to assess how people are experiencing the congregation. I have found narrative inquiry to be the best means for identifying the impact the congregation is having on people's lives. Please *do not* send out a congregational survey to garner this information. This is often interpreted to be a process for identifying what people prefer or desire within the congregation, for example, style of music or preaching, type of Bible studies or programs. It will not garner the type of deep thinking that you're looking for. Instead, invite specific people to tell their stories in video form that you can show during worship and post on the website.

For example, several years ago, while serving in my first congregation, I noticed a single mother whose giving had increased dramatically from one year to the next. Curious about this, I contacted her to ask about the increase. I was surprised to learn that she had taken seriously the call to tithing that we had promoted during the annual stewardship appeal. I asked whether she would be willing to share her story with the congregation. She told me that she wanted to wait a year to see what impact tithing would have on her life. At the end of the year, as we prepared for the next annual stewardship appeal, I reconnected with her, and she created the most powerful video testimony for tithing that I have ever witnessed. People wept openly as they listened to her story of courage and faith amid the challenges and struggles of raising her children alone. We never received more pledges and increases in giving than we did that year.

Pay attention to the people in your congregation who exemplify the congregation's culture and invite them to share stories about how they are living out the core values of the congregation and what difference this is making in their lives. Don't feel like these videos need to be filmed on expensive recording equipment. Because of social media, people today are accustomed to watching videos filmed on smartphones. The videos only need to be a minute or two of people sharing their experiences with the congregational culture. Not only will videos provide important qualitative information to the leadership, but they will encourage other members of the congregation to reflect on their experiences. They will also provide invitations for people on the periphery to become more engaged within the congregational culture. Showing videos of real people participating within the congregational culture and experiencing personal transformation as a result is an incredibly powerful tool for celebrating the strategic cultural development. It's important to identify and celebrate small successes as they occur, because it serves to generate positive energy toward further transformation.

You can see in this explanation of the strategic planning process the amount of work necessary for creating strategic focus and then executing and maintaining it. It is not easy. Because many pastors do not have the skills, experience, or understanding for such things, creating accompaniment relationships between vitalized, healthy congregations (with cultural architects serving as their pastors) and struggling congregations with high potential for development is the most effective path forward. The next chapter will discuss what such a model might look like.

5

ANCHOR CHURCH

It takes a village to raise a child.

—African proverb

When I graduated from seminary, I was called as a solo pastor to serve a small congregation outside Nashville, Tennessee. At the time, the congregation was thirteen years old and had an average worship attendance of about fifty. They had not had a full-time pastor for four years. The founding pastor had stayed for eleven years, but in his final two years was reduced to part-time status because the congregation was unable to pay him a full-time salary. They had a part-time interim pastor for the two years prior to my arrival. The assistant to the bishop told me when I accepted the call that my role was either to transform the congregation or close it. I had no idea what I was doing, but I went forward anyway.

Miraculously, the congregation grew rapidly. New people showed up, and in 2000, just six years after my arrival, our congregation was awarded the ELCA Evangelism Award for congregational development. Then conflict struck. Many of the original fifty members who were there when I arrived believed it was time for me to go because they felt displaced by the new people and the new congregational culture. Pastors who have experienced congregational conflict know firsthand the depth of pain and uncertainty it creates within themselves and the congregation. It's horrible. After an intervention from a synod-assigned conflict resolution task force, the angry group left the congregation, while those of us who remained took about a year to stay the course, rest, and recover before rolling up our sleeves to reengage in congregational development. I wish that I had had a mentoring pastor from a vitalized congregation nearby with whom our congregation would have had a deep relationship from the beginning of my ministry. I believe such support would have reinforced our development while also equipping me and our leaders to address the toxicities that existed just beneath the surface during those first five years. Such mentoring may have helped prevent the percolating anger from becoming full-blown conflict.

When Abiding Hope decided to partner with struggling congregations with high potential for development (see chap. 2), our hope from the start was to create a system that could be replicated throughout the greater church. Because congregational development is largely contextual, meaning there is no cookie-cutter model that will work in all circumstances, our system is based on identifying indigenous values to generate culture, rather than on a specific structure and design. Word of the anchor church movement has spread in the ELCA during the last year, and we are currently working to equip and train about fifteen congregations across the country to become anchor churches. Their individual stories are nothing short of inspiring.

For example, a congregation that we have been equipping in South Dakota, the second largest congregation in its synod, has developed a relationship with a struggling Native American (Lakota) congregation. The larger anchor church is discovering that such partnerships are not one-sided. On the contrary, when we create accompaniment relationships between congregations, both benefit. The larger congregation also went through the process of creating new guiding statements and is now in its own strategic planning phase as it accompanies the Lakota congregation to guide it in its cultural development. The relationship is proving to be mutually beneficial and life giving in that as the Lakota congregation is directly influencing the strategic direction of the larger congregation.

So it is with the accompaniment model of the anchor church movement. This model is based in a sense of humility, compassion, and service. If the anchor church views itself as the resident experts who've come to save the day for the struggling congregation, they've lost the very essence of what the accompaniment model seeks to accomplish, that is, mutual cultural development. Intentional relationships, by nature of what they are, transform both parties. Think about engaging in a relationship with a spouse or a close friend. Each person is affected because of the relationship. It's impossible to predict how being in relationship will change each party, but we know through experience that relationships transform all involved. Expectant parents get tired of people saying, "Just wait until the baby arrives. Your lives will never be the same." But it's true: a baby changes everything. Any congregation seeking to become an anchor church needs to recognize that the new relationship with another congregation will be transformative to your own congregational culture. That's a good thing, as long as the transformation is missionally focused and intentional.

The transformation begins with the anchor church going through the process of strategic cultural development prior to or concurrent with generating a relationship with a partner congregation. How can a student surgeon be mentored by someone who has never done surgery? How can a student teacher be mentored by someone who has never taught school? Don't assume that just because a congregation appears to be successful that it understands cultural architecture. It's important that the potential anchor church form its own vision team to engage the congregation in intentional cultural analysis before or concurrent to engaging in a relationship with others.

This can occur in many ways. First, if the potential anchor church has not engaged in a process to create effective guiding statements, or the current guiding statements are out of date or obsolete, this is a great place to begin (see chaps. 3–4). Going through the process to generate new guiding statements will equip the anchor church to mentor others. The same holds true for generating a new strategic plan. I have also seen positive examples of an anchor church and its partner congregations going through the processes of strategic cultural development concurrently. In fact, under the guidance of strong leadership, this can be an excellent way to establish mutual blessing and deepen the congregational relationship.

Second, if the anchor church already has effective guiding statements, then the vision team of the anchor church can help create a vision for how the congregation can live more fully into the guiding statements through an anchor church partnership.

This is what Abiding Hope did back in 2013–2014 through our visioning process. After the team assessed our guiding statements to be relevant and effective, we went to work to create the Abiding Hope Generous Life Vision (see appendix A). While we recognized that our guiding statements continued to be strong and relevant, we needed a new vision for living into the statements with greater efficacy and reach. The Generous Life Vision was as follows:

1. Increase our missional effectiveness

    a. Remain true north biblically and theologically, boldly broadcasting our unique message while continually demonstrating that all means *all*.
    b. Weave individual stories into God's story to form identity and purpose.
    c. Inspire the Abiding Hope community to be faithful in worship, consistently building relationships, involved in daily service, and practicing radical generosity.

2. Unite others to work as one in serving the world

    a. Partner with churches at risk of closing to raise them up again.
    b. Explore possibilities for creating worship and ministries that serve the growing Latino population of the Denver community.
    c. Expand our outreach and service both locally and globally.

3. Be a blessing to the greater church

    a. Establish an Abiding Hope leadership network.

      b. Create a publishing house to provide resources for other leaders, congregations, and organizations.

      c. Seek partnerships with diverse organizations that share a vision for the greater good.

Once the congregation approved this vision, the key leaders and I began to create a new strategic plan for how we would transform our culture to live into the vision. That same strategic plan continues to be updated and amended annually as we strive to achieve the vision set before us.

Ultimately, the anchor church movement exists to provide a medium for congregations to share with one another their best practices for cultural development, keeping in mind that what works in one place may not work in another. Through ongoing shared dialogue, we encourage one another, especially during times of failure or adversity (and there will be many), in addition to helping one another become more culturally aware and organizationally intelligent. The anchor church movement is also intended to become another tool in the judicatory toolbox for assisting struggling congregations. As I write this, about one-quarter of the congregations in the Rocky Mountain Synod of the ELCA are without a pastor. With our current clergy shortage, some may not be able to find a pastor. Anchor churches could be a way to address this situation as congregations come together to share staff and accompany one another toward cultural transformation.

As indicated by Russ Crabtree, about 90 percent of the congregations in our denomination are either maintaining or have crossed into the category of struggling.[1] The anchor church movement could become a strategy for helping a number of those struggling congregations to become revitalized. The beautiful thing about this model of accompaniment is its pay-it-for-

1. Crabtree, *State of the Evangelical Lutheran Church*, 25.

ward design. Once a formerly struggling congregation has become healthy and vitalized, it will have the opportunity to mentor others into the path of strategic cultural development. However, before we can move forward in creating anchor church partnerships, we must have a conversation regarding discernment.

Assessing Potential Anchor Churches

I must admit that currently I am unaware of any existing tools for assessing who has the capacity to become an anchor church. Please note that the size of the congregation or the congregation's staff should not be the defining factor in assessing this potential. Anchor churches will come in all shapes and sizes. The key factor is the culture of the congregation, not the size. The anchor church pastor must be a cultural architect who both is culturally aware and understands the processes for transforming a culture. Perhaps there is a pastor who was called into a conflicted congregation and, after five to seven years, a healthy and vitalized congregational culture emerged. Such a person would be a great candidate for the anchor church movement. Or consider a congregation in a small town that has seen pastors come and go, yet the congregation has a long history for vitality lived out through relationships and service into the greater community. Such a congregation would be a great candidate for the anchor church movement. Or perhaps there is a congregation that has been managing through the turbulent culture of the twenty-first century but just hasn't been able to cross the threshold into becoming vitalized. With some training and investment, the pastor and key leaders could be equipped to become more culturally aware and organizationally intelligent. Such a congregation would then also be a candidate for the anchor church movement.

We must first recognize the anchor church mentors, coaches, and leaders within each judicatory who will be charged with identifying and raising up anchor church pastors. I submit that this anchor church champion should not be a member of the judicatory staff but a practitioner in the field who is currently serving an anchor church. Certainly, this person works in concert with the judicatory staff in identifying new anchor churches and potential partners and in acquiring the necessary financial support for the movement. However, mentors and coaches for the movement must be practitioners who are cultural architects, as they live on the cutting edge of strategic cultural development.

One anchor church in our first cohort is Calvary Lutheran Church in Rapid City, South Dakota, the church I referred to above. It is the second largest congregation in the ELCA–South Dakota Synod. It had recently paid off the debt of a building expansion and was at a crossroads of trying to determine what was next. They were led by a husband and wife clergy couple who shared the lead pastor role. Both pastors were authentic and vulnerable in naming that they needed some guidance in organizational intelligence and strategic development as related to creating a new vision and direction for the congregation. Hearing about our work with three struggling congregations in the Denver community, the leaders of Calvary reached out to me, and we began the work of guiding them through the redevelopment process. After they went through the process of creating new guiding statements, you could see a renewed sense of identity and purpose.

The strategic planning phase opened a door for them to create a new partnership with a small, struggling Native American (Lakota) ELCA congregation not far from their location. This partnership, although relatively new (not even a year old), has invigorated both congregations. Calvary became an anchor church because it was seeking new identity and purpose, which resulted in its wanting to share its blessings and gifts with others.

Identifying pastors and congregations to serve as anchor churches at this time is somewhat subjective and thus will occur largely through relationships. Judicatory leaders and anchor church coaches/mentors should engage in conversation to discuss whom they know with the potential to become an anchor church. A list of potential persons should be generated and then vetted by the judicatory staff (they may have information about pastors or congregations that others don't have) before invitations are issued. The anchor church coach is responsible for generating a system for connecting and equipping anchor church pastors. The process that we've created thus far is as follows:

- Potential anchor church pastors and key leaders are invited to attend a gathering where the anchor church process is explained.

- The anchor church coach/mentor follows up individually with each participant of the gathering to assess interest and availability.

- The pastors who are interested in participating as an anchor church are formed into cohorts of ten to fifteen for ongoing training.

- A nine- to twelve-month training process is generated by the anchor church coach/mentor, which involves a one-hour, once-a-month Zoom conference to address

  ○ organizational intelligence,

  ○ cultural awareness,

- ○ process for generating guiding statements,
- ○ creating strategic plans, and
- ○ gallup's StrengthsFinder.

- Notice that there are only five key points included in the training. This allows for topics to be covered over a series of months, along with space for participants to share regarding their progress.

- The coach/mentor should also conduct one one-hour coaching session with each cohort participant per month.

Because of the time requirements (about 20 to 24 hours per month) for the anchor church coach/mentor, their congregation will need to be fully on board with the anchor church movement as a key component of the congregation's mission. One coach/mentor should be assigned for each cohort group, which means that as the movement evolves within the judicatory, more coaches/mentors will need to be identified and equipped. Once the pastors have completed the anchor church training, the judicatory leaders will recommend one to three partner congregations for each anchor church to accompany.

In my opinion, the role of the judicatory should be largely relational, in that the judicatory connects leaders and congregations with others who possess the resources or skills that aid congregational development. The judicatory cannot be the coaches or the supervisors or the experts in congregational vitality. Leave that to those actively serving congregations. However, the central office is necessary for the purposes of networking, vetting, and communicating. Ideally, a high level of trust would exist between congregational leaders and judicatory leaders so that no hierarchy surfaces, and there is recognition that each is uniquely gifted and positioned to accompany one another toward the common goal of congregational vitality.

Let's now explore how to identify and assess potential for partner congregations.

Assessing Partner Congregations

Because we have a limited number of anchor churches, it's essential that each partner congregation have high potential for development. The first aspect of assessing potential is to look at the data regarding the surrounding community. Is the population growing or declining? Has the population demographic shifted in recent years? What are the needs of the greater community? Does the congregation have the potential for addressing those needs? The assessor must then take a hard look at the pastor of the potential partner congregation. Does the potential partner currently have a pastor? Is the pastor capable of being equipped to become a cultural architect? Is the pastor emotionally and relationally healthy?

Not all congregations and not all pastors are able to be transformed. If we connect anchor churches to congregations that lack potential or are too toxic, we will drain the passion and energy for the movement. The assessment of potential partner congregations should involve both the leaders of the anchor church and judicatory leaders. Both parties should be free to speak honestly and candidly regarding potential partners so that red flags can be identified and potential solutions can be explored. For example, leaders of Abiding Hope recognized some red flags with the pastor of a potential partner congregation, and thus we asked the judicatory leaders to intervene before beginning the partnership. The members of the partner congregation concurred that a change would be best for all, and so the judicatory assisted the pastor in finding a new call so that the new accompaniment partnership could begin.

Another aspect for assessing potential partner congregations, one that is hugely significant for us in the ELCA, is identifying opportunities to generate vitalized congregations in communities of ethnic diversity. Sadly, the ELCA ranks as the whitest faith organization in the United States. ELCA data indicates that our denomination is about 98 percent white. This is due largely to Lutheranism being tied directly to western Europe, particularly Germany and Scandinavia. However, because the Lutheran faith has become culturally enmeshed with European lifestyles (e.g., food, music, dress, expression), Lutheran congregations in the United States have struggled greatly in reaching persons of different ethnicities.

Because the anchor church movement is focused primarily on cultural development, I believe it can become an effective tool for ethnic diversification. Again, such an approach needs to be intentional and thoughtful. The posture of the white congregation needs to begin with humility to create relationships with and listen to members of the surrounding community to discover both the needs of the community and ways in which a new, blended culture can be developed. Such relationships and listening processes take time. It's best to identify leaders in the ethnic community who can guide the congregation in relationship building and listening while generating opportunities to bring the whole community together. In my experience, the congregation will participate in shared service opportunities in the community before beginning to draw community members to worship or into other ministries. Trust must be established before any further development can occur. Community leaders who possess high relational capital within the neighborhood can help the congregation to establish such trust. However, the leaders of the congregation must be willing to be humble, to listen, and to be guided by the voices of the greater community.

Such listening might involve hearing how the greater community views or perceives the congregation, which isn't always pleasant. For instance, when working several years ago with an inner-city Lutheran congregation in Nashville, we heard from the largely African American neighborhood (which was formerly German) that many neighbors were offended when the congregation built a very high fence around their basketball court and kept the gate locked so that neighborhood kids couldn't use it. To be fair, windows in the church had been broken over the years, and graffiti would occasionally show up on the stone structure. However, the African American leaders told the congregational leaders that if the congregation were more welcoming and inclusive of the people in the neighborhood, the vandalism would probably occur less frequently. This information was tough to hear, and some in the congregation attempted to rationalize the fencing and the invisible walls that had been created. Ultimately, the congregation sought to become a better neighbor to the surrounding community, which led to steps toward revitalization.

As the United States becomes more ethnically diverse, congregations can become leaders within the community, assisting in greater cultural development. However, this will only occur if congregational leaders are intentional in becoming cultural architects. The intent is for the congregational culture of life and vitality to spill over into the surrounding neighborhood as people are drawn into the life-giving values of the Jesus community. People don't necessarily need to become members of the congregation to live the congregation's culture. As community members participate in a community garden sponsored by the congregation, or are served by a drop-in day care program for older adults, or their kids receive tutoring, or they attend a free community meal once a week, the values and culture of the congregation will undoubtedly affect people's daily lives. Judicatories should place a high priority for identifying potential partner congregations within ethnically diverse communities, because this is the future of the American landscape.

As Abiding Hope has accompanied Christ the King, which resides in a neighborhood that is 72 percent Latino, our largely white, upper-middle-class constituency has become more engaged in generating relationships with the Latino community. These relationships help us to be better equipped to address issues such as systemic racism, immigration, economic development, and education for those for whom English is a second language. These experiences create within us a deeper sense of compassion and love for our Latino brothers and sisters, which plays out in how we vote, how we use our gifts in service of others, and how we raise our kids to be in relationship with persons of a variety of ethnicities and backgrounds. These relationships not only serve to create a new congregational culture, but they are leading to the generation of a new American culture of greater inclusion and cooperation. Until people of different ethnicities can coexist in peace and mutual blessing, the church has much work to do, and I believe it begins with local congregations.

Beyond assessing the developmental capacity of the congregation, the pastor of the potential partner congregation needs to have the capacity to become a cultural architect. For this to occur, the person needs to be

- emotionally and relationally healthy;

- teachable and able to integrate information well and apply it to daily routines;

- humble enough to recognize and accept where past practices have failed;

- bold enough to trust that they can become an effective leader;

- willing to submit to the coaching of the anchor church pastor and the leadership of the vision team; and

- courageous to take risks, to stand up to conflict and pushback, and to be consistent in leading the congregation forward.

If any of these attributes are not present, the pastor will become a roadblock to the strategic cultural development of the partner congregation. If the pastor cowers under the pressure of toxic people who complain and threaten to build a coalition against the new cultural development, the revitalization plan will be put in great jeopardy. This will not only derail the transformative process, but it will greatly diminish the trust capital of the congregation for the anchor church's leadership.

If a pastor is in place who does not possess the attributes identified above, that person will need to leave before an accompaniment partnership can occur. Removing the pastor will require assistance from the judicatory and the approval of the congregation. As the anchor church bears no authority or power within the partner congregation, it will be necessary for the judicatory to intervene. Of course, the congregation must agree virtually unanimously with the need for the pastor to leave. A representative from the bishop's office should be the one to facilitate such conversations with the pastor, the congregation council, and the congregation. The easiest path is to ask for the pastor's resignation. Typically, if the pastor recognizes that her leadership has become ineffective and that the majority of the congregation desires a change, she will tender her resignation. If the pastor refuses to resign, the congregation may be forced to vote to remove the pastor. Such occurrences are always painful, so seeking a more amicable solution is preferred. However, let's remember that the health and vitality of the congregation is the most important issue here, not the employment of the pastor.

I strongly recommend that the anchor church assist in ensuring that the pastor being removed is treated with dignity and respect. That person should receive a generous severance package as well as the continuation of benefits until they receive a new call. Their dismissal from the congregation should not create a financial burden for them or undue difficulties for their family aside from moving. Once again, though, we must remember that the health and vitality of the congregation is the main focus, and no congregation should be held captive to a pastor who does not possess the set of gifts needed to lead the congregation's revitalization. None of us has a right to be a pastor. Serving as pastor is a call from God, and congregations deserve to be led by pastors who are well-equipped to guide them toward health and vitality. The anchor church movement is intended to participate along with seminaries and judicatories in equipping pastors to become effective cultural architects, leading congregations toward health and vitality.

Creating the Anchor Church Partnership

Once the judicatory identifies the partner congregations for the anchor church and all agree to move forward, the first step is to create a covenant. I've included as appendix C the covenant we created for our relationship with Christ the King, because it is the most extensive in substance. The covenant needs to clearly define the relationship between the anchor church and the partner congregation. When we began our partnership, Christ the King did not have a pastor (he was asked to resign prior to the start of the partnership), and thus we used Abiding Hope staff in service of Christ the King. Not only did this arrangement give us greater control in developing the new culture at Christ the King, but it provided an enormous financial break to Christ the King during the beginning stages of development. The covenant was made available to the people of Christ the King so that they could vote either to accept or reject it. We convened several public forums prior to the vote to answer questions and quell any concerns. The synod's director for evangelical mission was on hand at the forums, as well as the gathering for the vote, to affirm the synod's role in the process. By the time of the vote, everyone was ready to move forward with the new partnership.

If other partnerships are not to be as intense as the Abiding Hope–Christ the King relationship, the covenant should reflect the nature of the partnership, define the power or leadership structures, and indicate what success will look like. Perhaps the partnership is simply to create guiding statements and a new strategic plan, while providing coaching of the pastor and leaders. This would all be described in detail within the covenant. Do not cut corners. Be careful to think through anything that could potentially create problems in the partnership so that it can be included in the covenant.

During the relationship with Abiding Hope, the covenant serves as our primary governing document, not Christ the King's constitution. Technically, the constitution still exists, but for the sake of redevelopment, it is shelved for a designated period of time so that the guiding coalition, which we call the vision team, is empowered to be nimble in making strategic decisions. Once the congregation becomes healthy and vitalized, the vision team will reexamine the constitution to discern changes that need to occur to match the new congregational culture. For instance, the congregation may decide not to return to a twelve-member council but instead maintain a seven-member leadership team. Such a change would need to be noted within the constitution. There will undoubtedly be other necessary amendments to defining the key committees or teams necessary to the ongoing strategic cultural development.

Once the covenant is approved by all parties and the partnership begins, the vision team then engages in the necessary work to generate trust through relationship building. The team also assesses what needs require immediate attention (e.g., care for shut-ins, financial management, worship life, sustaining existing ministries) and the best media by which to communicate with the membership. The vision team is also charged with creating a timeline and plan to begin the process of generating new guiding statements, followed by a strategic plan (see chap. 4). I recommend that this process begin within the first three to six months of the partnership. The anchor church lead pastor is charged with coaching the pastor of the partner congregation, equipping the vision team in healthy practices, and navigating through all the necessary processes by utilizing organizational intelligence.

At this point, there is no cookie-cutter concept for what will occur. Every context is different. Every congregation is different. Leaders must stay focused on the strategic cultural development and be able to roll with the ebbs and flows. Every ounce of emotional and relational intelligence will be tested, so it helps if the leaders are versed in Dr. Murray Bowen's family systems theory. Leaders must consistently be nonanxious as they navigate through turbulent waters and look for win-win solutions to conflict. The best way to do this is for the vision team to support one another, stand together as a united front, have one another's backs, and collaborate on all decisions. It's the role of the anchor church pastor to help buttress the pastor and leaders of the partner congregation through any instances of conflict, which will occur. But when handled in a healthy manner, conflict can serve to define the vision more clearly while garnering trust from the membership.

I am excited to see what sorts of innovative congregational cultures and ministries can be developed through the anchor church movement. I believe that when we remove fear through mutually beneficial relationships, the Holy Spirit breaks in to create new life, transcending our wildest imaginations. The next chapter will explore other anchor church models that demonstrate such innovative development.

6

OTHER ANCHOR CHURCH MODELS

The true sign of intelligence is not knowledge
but imagination.

—Albert Einstein

I am writing primarily about the accompaniment model of
anchor church because that is the model with which I am most
experienced. However, there are other models for anchor
church that deserve equal attention and will require someone
more experienced than I to write about them. My intent now
is simply to give some basic information about other models so
that you, the reader, can be informed. As the anchor church
movement is still in its infancy, I am just now learning of practitioners for each of these examples. You may want to peruse the

congregations in your area, district, conference, or synod to see who is engaging in this sort of work so that you can glean some wisdom and insight from their experiences.

Poly-Site Model

I'd like to begin with the poly-site model because we have recently begun to experiment with this concept at Abiding Hope. I believe that the future is going to reveal a movement toward smaller communities of people who intentionally choose to do life together as church. Their regular gatherings will include some form of worship, life sharing, service, generosity, food, and relationship building. These groups of ten to thirty people will meet in a variety of places, such as homes, brewpubs, coffee shops, or even out in nature. They won't need a church building and probably won't ever enter a church building. However, they will need an anchor church for stability, accountability, resources, training, and connection to greater community. I envision the leaders of each group being trained and equipped by the anchor church pastor. The group leaders will serve as pastor to their group, creating the agendas and liturgies for their weekly gatherings, presiding at baptisms and Communion, and providing detailed reports of the progress of their group to the anchor church. Periodically, the anchor church might host events to gather all the groups together for relationship building and generating greater community. But for the most part, the individual poly-site groups will function individually as they seek to draw one another into living the shared values of Christ.

We call this model poly-site versus multisite because each individual group will be different and unique, living the culture generated by its particular collection of people. The term *multi-site* has come to represent the traditional congregational model with multiple locations. The prefix *poly–* has a Greek origin meaning *many*, as in the term *polymerous*, meaning "many parts." A poly-site congregation isn't simply a congregation with multiple sites; it's a congregation of multiple sites that are part of one another, while being quite different from one another. The aim of each poly-site group is not growth but going deeper in generating authentic relationships with one another. When new people are joining all the time, it changes the dynamics of the existing communities. Poly sites won't grow; they'll multiply. One site can launch another site or be a resource for a newly developing site. Remember, the goal is life, and life is generated through intentional immersion into values. It takes time for such authentic communities to develop and thrive.

Another version or aspect for the poly-site model is a congregation that creates different structures or organizations for serving the greater community. For instance, a congregation might decide to convert a storefront nearby into a help center that provides food, clothing, and toiletries to those in need. Or maybe a congregation builds a skate park on their property to engage local teenagers and provides adult guides and leaders who build relationships with the teens. Some might call this a ministry of the congregation, and certainly it is, but we're hoping to generate a deeper conversation about cultural architecture, not only within the congregation but out into the greater community. Poly-site ministries can serve to accomplish such purposes. The people who visit the help center or the kids who use the skate park may never step foot into the church's worship center or facility, and yet they are being affected by the culture of Christ through interaction with the poly-site ministries.

While we at Abiding Hope have experimented with a pub ministry and a coffeehouse ministry, I would not yet categorize them as poly-site. Our hope is to begin to generate several poly-site groups throughout the greater Denver community beginning in 2020. We also hope to explore what other similar systems are being developed by others. We still have much to learn, but I believe that there is tremendous potential in the poly-site model, especially for reaching the millennial generation, and hope that we can cut through some of the denominational red tape to give permission for these groups to do organic ministry together.

Adoption Model

I don't profess to be an expert or practitioner of the adoption model for anchor church. It was generated by my good friend Scott Suskovic, lead pastor of Christ Lutheran Church in Charlotte, North Carolina. Much of what follows regarding the adoption model was created by Scott. I am grateful that he has given me permission to include his concepts in this book.

The adoption model is built out of a both/and mindset, as it seeks to create a new congregational family by bringing struggling congregations under the umbrella of a larger, vitalized congregation. According to Scott, this approach envisions a model that is not based on several campuses that all look and sound the same, as seen with some megachurches, where one preacher is live-streamed to several locations. Neither does it envision a synodical model where congregations are in loose partnership with one another. The adoption model would be a both/and single congregational approach, with multiple campuses having

- unity as one congregation *but* freedom of different expressions,

- common branding *but* individual look,

- centralized membership *but* pastoral responsibility for sites,
- centralized finances *but* campus stewardship,
- one staff *but* sharing resources,
- one leadership team *but* individual decision-making,
- common goals *but* individual accountability,
- one council *but* campus representation, and
- one overall vision *but* campus discernment teams.

According to Scott, there are four criteria to consider when an anchor church ponders adopting a struggling congregation into its organization. First, the congregation must be located in an area with potential for growth and within a reasonable distance of the anchor church—ideally less than a half-hour driving distance. Unfortunately, there are many congregations that could use the help of an anchor church, but as we launch this movement, we must be intentional to adopt those that are located in areas of high potential for growth.

Second, the congregation must be vacant of a pastor. Just as with the accompaniment model, the adoption model seeks to transform the culture of the struggling congregation. However, unlike the accompaniment model, the struggling congregation will now become an ongoing part of the anchor church. Therefore, the preferred method is to begin with a new pastoral leader who can embody the developing culture and values of the anchor church. It is extraordinarily difficult to retrain a pastor out of a toxic culture into a new, vitalized culture. Thus, starting with new pastoral leadership is preferred.

Third, the partner congregation must be eager to engage holistically in the adoption. Pay close attention if there is any level of reticence in the partner congregation for engaging in the new relationship. There should not need to be a tremendous amount of convincing or urging for the new partnership to occur. If the spirit of willingness and boldness is not there, it is best not to enter into the partnership, because the reticence will undoubtedly return, most likely in unhealthy ways, when changes begin to occur.

Fourth, the congregation must be willing to pay the price. This is the most difficult and expensive price to pay. Every church says that it wants to grow, but few are willing to rethink their mission and ministry. The price tag includes

- renaming of the congregation;

- infusing a new culture;

- financial oversight and property ownership by the anchor church;

- change of worship style and programming;

- change of branding;

- disbanding of congregational council;

- increasing expectations of volunteering, inviting, giving, and outreach;

- intentional movement from operating out of survival to thriving out of strengths.

Scott also explains,

The words that provide value to our understanding of this partnership are *unity* and *autonomy*. There will be unity of staff, membership, vision, council, and finances while allowing for autonomy of expression in programming, evangelism, outreach, and worship. Pastors from all campuses will be called by the anchor church with specific responsibilities to a specific campus or campuses. To assist these lead campus pastors, hand-picked discernment teams will provide direction and counsel to implement the overall vision into the specific context. This will shape worship, education, evangelism, and programming that is both concurrent with the overall vision and specific to that particular campus.

You can see from Scott's description regarding the adoption model that the struggling congregations become a part of the anchor church entity, while maintaining contextually specific missional focus. Scott's congregation, Christ Lutheran in Charlotte, has been engaged in this work for about three years, and while it has doubled the size of the once-struggling congregation, this is one of the most difficult ministries to execute successfully. Many who are involved in this type of ministry report that it will take a minimum of three to five years to see a significant turnaround. The difficulties lie in changing the culture from within the congregation while also transforming the outside community's perception of the congregation's culture. From within, there is often a culture of scarcity and fear that is difficult to reimagine and revision. From outside, the surrounding community already has a perception that this church is stuck and struggling. To engage the outside community, great effort is required to transform the myopic congregational mindset from within so that new engagement with the surrounding community can occur.

In addition, the adoption model can also be employed for new starts. While transforming the culture of a small, struggling congregation, Christ Lutheran also launched a new worshipping community in a local school with the same intentional vision of organizational unity through promoting autonomy in cultural development. Starting from a blank slate is arguably easier than transforming a dysfunctional culture. But what makes this model more desirable than the traditional denominational parachute drop of mission development is that the campus pastor at the partner congregation is freed from the administrative, financial, and personnel tasks that are all covered by the anchor church. This affords the campus pastor more time to engage people and invest in the cultural architecture. In addition, the campus pastor has the support of the resources, coaching, leadership, and vision of the anchor church. Instead of the campus pastor being a single mission developer, she is now part of a larger community and team to aid in key decisions and to provide ongoing coaching and collaboration.

The adoption model is worth exploring in many of our urban and suburban contexts where significant demographic changes have occurred over recent decades. It's also a model that could be used as an incubator in shaping future cultural architects who can then be called to serve in potential anchor churches.

Franchise Model

The final model for anchor church is what we are calling the franchise model. Admittedly, I have no experience with such a model but know that it exists and thus want to draw attention to it. The one that comes to mind for me is Hope Lutheran Church in West Des Moines, Iowa, under the leadership of Pastor Mike Householder. Much like franchises with which we are familiar (e.g., McDonald's, Walmart, Target, Costco), when you've seen one, you've seen them all. I don't have to worry about the recipe used for a Big Mac in Ohio versus Colorado. I know what to expect from one McDonald's to the next. So it is with the franchise model for congregational development.

Similar to the adoption model above, the franchise model will have multiple sites for its congregation. But different from the adoption model, each site of the franchise will be nearly the same in terms of branding, feel, worship, and culture. Often the preacher of the franchise model is live-streamed into worship at each of the sites to ensure uniformity and consistency. While each site might have its own worship leader or site pastor, the worship life and the ministry development will look the same at each site.

We tend to see franchise-model congregations develop in urban and suburban settings, because they tend to generate in areas of rapid population growth and economic development. If a struggling congregation were to be brought into a franchise-model anchor church, that congregation would experience a holistic facelift of its facility so that it resembled the anchor church. There would be a complete overhaul of the staff, because the leadership would be provided by the anchor church. A positive example of this franchise model is Adam Hamilton's work through the United Methodist Church of the Resurrection in Leawood, Kansas. Currently operating with five campuses, several of these were small or medium-sized churches that were taken over by the parent or anchor church and transformed into its version of the franchise model. In fact, almost all of the numerical growth that this congregation, the largest congregation of the United Methodist Church in the United States, has experienced in the past ten years has been through acquiring small congregations and helping them to become vitalized once again.

While I've outlined four basic models for anchor church, there are countless other possible variations on each model. Some are doing the franchise model but with a campus pastor who also preaches. Some use the adoption model but have a single preaching pastor for all sites, either live-streamed or recorded. The poly-site model might be two congregations of equal size sharing space, overhead expenses, or staff. And the accompaniment model allows for a variety of relationships between the anchor church and partner congregations depending on the needs of each. There is no one model that is better than another; as we have examples for how each can be successful in creating healthy, vitalized congregational culture.

If we are going to envision a new church for a new time, we need to tap into the abundance of resources, creativity, leadership, and vision provided by congregations that are currently healthy and strong. It's time to embrace the blessings of the Spirit within healthy congregations while bringing their visionary leaders together to encourage collaboration, innovation, and creativity. Undoubtedly, new models and systems leading to congregational vitality will be developed as the Spirit guides us in our journey. I look forward to what lies ahead through trust in our creative, resurrecting God, who brings new life into every situation of darkness or death. To God be the glory.

Epilogue: What's Next?

If you never want to be criticized,
for goodness' sake don't do anything new.

—Jeff Bezos

If you read the Abiding Hope Generous Life Vision (see appendix A), you'll notice that in addition to becoming an anchor church that accompanies struggling congregations toward health and vitality, we feel called to create a leadership network, along with resources to assist others in their strategic cultural development. We are currently in the process of accomplishing both goals. The very first anchor church cohort includes thirteen ELCA pastors from around the country who are participating in training to advance the work they're currently doing or to become an anchor church. This is just the beginning. Through the support of the ELCA, we will be convening periodic gatherings around the country to inform others and invite them into the anchor church movement. Not everyone who attends one of our gatherings will become an anchor church. However, we're seeking to get the word out so the movement can grow and develop organically.

In the meantime, Abiding Hope is working to launch a web-based resource page to which pastors and leaders can subscribe to download all sorts of information and materials that will serve the cultural development within their congregations. Watch for this resource page to appear on www.abiding-hope.org. These resources will include podcasts that address various aspects of strategic cultural development, which can then be shared with congregational leaders as pastors work to transform their congregation's culture. The site will also provide examples for how to integrate guiding statements into worship themes or small groups as a way of enculturating the community. The resources will be divided into up-to-date materials (e.g., worship series, small group curricula, youth and family engagement) that can be easily used within the subscriber's congregation, as well as archives that can be searched to find specific materials or information. We want the network and resources to be relationship based, where everyone can participate in ongoing dialogue as we seek to be mutual blessings to one another.

Additionally, we hope to engage seminaries in conversations about the anchor church movement so that pastoral interns can be placed in anchor churches for a two-year contextual education experience focused on strategic cultural development. We envision seminaries becoming incubators for raising up cultural architects. Imagine pastors and leaders spending a week or two in residence at a seminary, where they would receive hands-on coaching and instruction in the area of cultural development, would then be assigned into an ongoing discussion cohort with their peers from the seminary event, and then be accompanied for at least the next twelve months by their cohort and coach. I realize that twelve months is not a very long time, but we have to start somewhere. I can see these cohort relationships volunteering to extend to three, four, even five years, because it takes this long (or longer) to transform a culture.

Finally, my hope is that denominations will think seriously about transforming their structures to be more effective in congregational development. When the ELCA was formed in 1987–88, the threefold expressions were created from theology built on the ontological Trinity, that is, three coequal parts: churchwide, synod, and congregation. I believe that those who created such a structure missed the mark, because the three expressions of the church are not coequal, as the three persons of the Trinity are. If holding to a Trinitarian formula is important and necessary, let's build the structure of the denomination out of a theology of the economic Trinity, that is, the way in which God functions. Father is God, the unoriginated One, in whom the Son and the Spirit originate and from whom the Son and Spirit are sent to draw all things to the Father. In other words, the Son and Spirit serve the mission of the Father, which is what makes God three in one.

As we think about congregations, judicatories, and the denomination, the three are not coequal or even conecessary. We can have congregation without judicatory or denomination. We can't have judicatory or denomination without congregations. Congregational vitality must be the primary and leading focus of every judicatory and denomination, for without healthy, vitalized congregations, no denominations will exist. What would it look like to put congregations at the top of the pyramid, with judicatories and the greater church beneath them to support, invest in, and encourage congregational development?

One hope I have in writing this book is that we can begin an honest and open church-wide conversation regarding transforming our structure to support congregational development.

This would involve making funds and resources easily accessible to anchor churches as they engage in redeveloping struggling congregations. Due to a culture of distrust within our denomination, the application process for funds and the required reporting procedures for how funds are used has become a deterrent to congregations partnering with the greater church. I have had countless pastors from larger congregations say it's not worth their time to try to work with the synod or denomination because of all the red tape and need for oversight and control. Surely, we can create a culture of high trust that results in processes and procedures that are easily followed and enable highly effective leaders to be enlisted in the anchor church movement. If not, larger congregations will continue to be lone wolves seeking to generate missional health and vitality on their own. Isn't it time to bridge the gap between our proven congregational leaders and the leaders of the denomination toward the shared vision of congregational vitality?

Finally, as judicatories and denominations are transformed, let's encourage participation in activities and events that produce lasting transformation of leaders and congregations. Local conference gatherings should be strategic in nature by fostering a shared mission between neighboring pastors and congregations, while also providing necessary support for maintaining focus on cultural development, especially during times of conflict. The topics for discussion should relate directly to forming cultural architects and should be led by persons with proven experience in transforming congregations. Simply getting together to share experiences or to conduct a book study will not result in lasting transformation, either personally or congregationally. Local conferences and synods, as well as the greater church, need to be far more intentional in defining what mutual investment looks like as it relates to strategic cultural development.

If something in this book has stirred the Spirit within you and you'd like to go deeper but don't know where to turn, reach out to us at Abiding Hope. Take a look at our website (www.abidinghope.org) and review our staff list. Feel free to contact any one of us directly by either phone or email. We'd love to engage you in conversation about your ministry context and help direct you to other resources. We can include you in our leadership network and connect you to others with whom you can engage in ongoing dialogue about strategic cultural development in your congregation. If you're looking for a coach or guide, we can help you in that regard also, because our network of coaches expands all across the country.

Finally, if you'd like to come to Littleton, Colorado, to experience firsthand what we do at Abiding Hope, we'd love to have you. We are blessed to serve in one of the most beautiful settings in the world, just at the base of the Rocky Mountains. Whether you come in the winter or the summer, there is always a lot to do in Colorado. While you enjoy nature, you will be immersed in our congregational culture to experience the sorts of things that will aid you in becoming a cultural architect. Even after you return home to your context, we will continue to be accessible to you for guidance and coaching. Again, you can learn more about opportunities such as these on our website.

Thank you for taking the time to read this book. While it certainly isn't exhaustive in any way, it's been created to be a blessing to all those engaged in congregational ministry and to add to the conversation regarding congregational vitality. May God bless you and your congregation as you strive to draw people into closer relationships with God, one another, and creation.

Appendix A: Abiding Hope Generous Life Vision (2015)

Where We've Been

Abiding Hope was formed as a faith community in 1987.

In 2010, we developed our new mission and vision statements and tagline.

We have set the stage for our future in many areas as

- one of the fifty largest ELCA congregations and the fourth-largest ELCA congregation giving to ministries beyond our doors;

- the founding congregation of the Haitian Timoun Foundation;

- the leading congregational partner with Trinity Lutheran Seminary;

- the founding congregation of a second site, which later became Well of Hope, a congregation under development; and

- having invested in over twenty pastoral interns.

Appendix A

Where We're Going

Our guiding statements continue to be effective and relevant:

- **Core values:** Authentic worship, intentional relationships, sacrificial service, radical generosity
- **Mission statement:** Equip all to be the heart, hands, and feet of Jesus in the world
- **Vision statement:** A wholly unleashed faith community
- **Tagline:** Experience real life

God is now counting on Abiding Hope to lead and equip other congregations and organizations in being the heart, hands, and feet of Jesus in the world. How will we do that?

1. Increase our missional effectiveness

    a. Remain true north biblically and theologically, boldly broadcasting our unique message while continually demonstrating that all means *all*.
    b. Weave individual stories into God's story to form identity and purpose.
    c. Inspire the Abiding Hope community to be faithful in worship, consistently building relationships, involved in daily service, and practicing radical generosity.

2. Unite others to work as one in serving the world

    a. Partner with struggling congregations with high potential toward revitalization.

b. Explore partnership possibilities with the growing Latino population of Denver.

c. Expand our outreach and service both locally and globally.

3. Be a blessing to the greater church

a. Establish a national leadership network for mutual investment and accountability.

b. Create a publishing house to provide resources for other leaders, congregations, and organizations.

c. Seek partnerships with organizations sharing our vision for the greater good.

Abiding Hope History

In 1987, a group of people led by Pastor Chris Brekke and passionate for serving God in southwest metro Denver formed Abiding Hope Lutheran Church. After gathering at Deer Creek Middle School for three years, the congregation moved into our new building at the corner of Coal Mine and Simms in 1990. God blessed Abiding Hope with rapid growth, and in 1993 we called Pastor Rick Barger to lead us into our new chapter of missional development. In 1997, the congregation added a new worship center and administration building. Recognizing a need to better serve the children, youth, and young adults of the community, Abiding Hope added the discipleship training center in 2003. The congregation adopted a lead-team model in 2004 in order to effectively serve our continually growing missional demands. On Christmas Eve 2007, the inaugural worship service of Abiding Hope's second site was held at Redstone Elementary School in Highlands Ranch. Pastor Rick Barger departed Abiding Hope in September 2008, resulting in Glenn Hecox, Pastor Doug Hill, and Pastor Chad Johnson being affirmed to continue as the lead team. In 2010, we convened a vision team, which developed new guiding statements consisting of core values and mission and vision statements, along with the tagline "Experience real life." In partnership with the Rocky Mountain Synod, Abiding Hope Redstone relocated to Castle Pines and in 2012 became a congregation under development for the ELCA, called a new pastor, and adopted the name Well of Hope.

Abiding Hope has been recognized as the fourth-largest congregation formed in the past thirty years and one of the fifty largest congregations in the ELCA. Abiding Hope is currently fourth in the ELCA in giving to ministries beyond our doors. We are the founding congregation of the Haitian Timoun Foundation and the leading congregational partner with Trinity Lutheran Seminary. We have been blessed to invest in nearly twenty pastoral interns, who currently serve in a variety of leadership roles throughout the greater church. We have formed countless ministries locally and globally proclaiming the good news of the risen Jesus and freeing people to live fully as children of God. We are known throughout the greater church as a place where the gifts of God are free and all means *all*! Oh Jesus, thank you for this place that is always filled with your grace.

Current Cultural Trends

According to data from the Barna Group, 75 percent of American adults claim to be looking for ways to live a more meaningful life, while 40 percent say that they don't need the church to find it.[1] The fastest growing religious demographic group is what Barna labels as "nones," those who reject any form of conventional description for their religious affiliation. As a result,

---

1. "Three Trends on Faith, Work and Calling," Barna Group, February 11, 2014, https://tinyurl.com/rez73dc.

worship attendance in Christian congregations across the country has been dramatically decreasing over the past fifteen years. According to a recent report in the *Lutheran Magazine*, ELCA average worship attendance went from 149 in 2000 to 111 in 2013.

Another significant trend within the church is the movement toward experiential theological reflection as opposed to cognitive understanding of doctrine. Persons today seek less to be told what the Bible means and instead desire to connect the content of Scripture with their own life experience. The movement toward subjective faith interpretation affects how we worship, study, and engage matters of spirituality within the life of the church. Creating opportunities for shared narrative within every aspect of our life together is essential for helping people to connect with God and one another.

Appendix B: Abiding Hope Systematic Theology and Ecclesiology

I have created this systematic theology (talk about God) and ecclesiology (talk about the church) for use by our leadership. This was not created for publication but to be used as a tool for articulating the Abiding Hope message in every aspect of our life together. I include the Abiding Hope systematic theology and ecclesiology purely as an example for creating clarity within a congregation regarding hermeneutical and theological grounding. I'm not suggesting that every congregation must espouse the theology/ecclesiology of Abiding Hope. I'm simply making the case that congregations that are clear in their theological foundation are on a path toward vitality. My aim is to offer our document as an example for how to generate such a resource.

Theological Overview and Hermeneutic

Hermeneutics is the lens by which we interpret Scripture and the many aspects of theology. Everyone has a hermeneutic. If you believe that God is angry because of the flaws of humanity and that Jesus was sent to be a pure, atoning sacrifice so that human beings who believe properly can go to heaven, you will read all of Scripture through such a lens. It's critically important to recognize and identify that at Abiding Hope we read and interpret Scripture through the lens of a particular hermeneutic, and our theology and ecclesiology is built on this hermeneutic.

The Abiding Hope hermeneutic is best described as a messianic apocalyptic eschatology. Let's address each term individually to gain a clear understanding of the collective meaning. *Messiah* is a Hebrew word that literally means "anointed one." The Greek equivalent is Christ (*Christos*). The first occurrence of the term *messiah* in Scripture is in 1 Samuel, when Samuel anoints Saul to be the first king of the Hebrew people; thus the terms *messiah* and *king* are linked together throughout Scripture and largely interchangeable. When we read 1 Samuel closely, we discover that God warns the people against having a messiah/king (1 Sam 8). But the people do not listen to God's warnings and insist that God provide for them an anointed one to be their king. As a result, God declares to the people through Samuel, "And in that day you will cry out because of your king, whom you have chosen for yourselves; but the Lord will not answer you in that day" (1 Sam 8:18).

It's critically important that we recognize that having a human messiah/king is not God's plan and is thus a dangerous phenomenon because it negatively affects human culture by necessarily creating social hierarchies. Whenever you have someone at the top, you necessarily have others at the bottom. Such a hierarchical system is counter to God's vision of oneness for all of humanity. As a result, we must note that Jesus never self-identifies in any of the four Gospels with either the title *messiah* or *king*. This absence of Jesus proclaiming to be the Messiah has been labeled as "the messianic secret" of the Gospels. On the contrary, Jesus wasn't keeping his messianic identity a secret per se; rather, he understood that such a nomenclature would automatically and immediately elevate him over his fellow human beings.

At the same time, it is important that we recognize Jesus as the true Messiah/King, for he is indeed God's anointed one who comes to usher in a new human culture. What differentiates Jesus from all other messiahs/kings before him is that he dies for his people, thus bringing an end to the hierarchical human structures created in 1 Samuel. We look to Jesus as *the* Messiah/King who brings an end to the old moral order governed by hierarchy, division, fear, and death in order to inaugurate a new moral order governed by oneness, inclusion, love, and life.

The term *apocalyptic* (from the Greek *apokalypsis*) literally means to "reveal, unveil, or uncover." When speaking biblically/theologically, we can take this word in a couple of ways. The first is that the term *apocalypse* uncovers or discloses a new age, a new way of being for humanity. The second is that the apocalypse uncovers or unveils the true identity for humanity. When we use the term *apocalyptic*, we are saying that through the person of Jesus and through his life, death, and resurrection, a new humanity and a new way of life have been unveiled or uncovered. This new identity is that human beings exist as children of God, and our true way of life is to be in oneness with God and one another. This demands inclusion and love for all.

Finally, the word *eschatology* is derived from the Greek term *eschaton*, which means "the final and culminating outcome of history." For us, the eschatological moment was the death and resurrection of Jesus, which birthed the new humanity. When we are baptized, we are baptized into the eschaton, put to death and raised anew as new human beings. Thus, when we say that we hold to a messianic apocalyptic eschatology, we are saying that we believe that a new humanity and a new age of inclusion for all people (the gifts of God are free, and all means *all!*) have been unveiled and birthed through the death and resurrection of Jesus, and we now are freed to live as citizens of this new reality. All of our theology and ecclesiology at Abiding Hope is developed through the lens of this messianic apocalyptic eschatology.

Who Is God?

God is the originator, creator, and source of all life. All that exists came into being through God (Gen 1–2). God is *agapē* (love; 1 John 4:8). God creates life out of love, to love, and for love. Love is the very essence and energy of life that flows through all things. God is inherently relational, serving, and generous. God self-identifies to Moses as one in relationship to Moses's ancestors, who serves the Hebrew people, and who continually provides for all their needs (Gen 12:1–3; Exod 3:6; 20:1–17; Josh 24:14–18). God sends Jesus, the enfleshment of the Logos (John 1:1–18), to draw humanity into relationship with God; God sends the Holy Spirit (John 14:25–31) to pour love into humanity and to draw humanity into relationship with God; and God sends the church (John 20:19–22) to be the in-Spirited vessel drawing humanity into relationship with God.

What Is the *Missio Dei* ("God's Mission") in the World?

The mission of God is to draw all things into intimate relationship (full communion) with God (John 12:27–32). The Holy Trinity is not to be understood solely as a static definition of God within God's own self (ontological Trinity) but viewed as an unfolding story of God's ongoing interaction with creation and humanity (economic Trinity). The Father is God, the source and creator of all things (Gen 1–2). The Son is the idea in the mind of God (the Light of the first day of Creation; Greek *logos/sophia*) for creation and humanity who becomes enfleshed in the person of Jesus of Nazareth, sent from the Father to draw all things to God (John 1:1–18). The Holy Spirit proceeds from the Father and the Son as God's creative force/energy (love) to empower humanity to work to draw all things to God (John 16:7–15).

What Are Human Beings?

Human beings are created *imago Dei*, in the image of God (Gen 1:26–27). The *imago Dei* is the ability to

- be aware of self and the "other," both God and human;

- experience the other through the senses while reflecting on self and other;

- have response-ability—relating to and serving the other; and

- engage in both differentiation and unity.

Human beings are creatures of the earth (*adamah*), intimately connected to the physical world (Gen 2:7, 18–25). The very substances that exist in the mountains, trees, seas, and animals exist in us. Humans stand as God-creatures, both *imago Dei* and *adamah*. As such, God calls and trusts humanity to be partners with God in creating life and forming the cosmos, which is to be understood as both the ordered systems of human culture and the natural world (Gen 1:28–31). As such, God entrusts humanity with the care of the creation. God respects humanity in our role and does not interfere in the formation of human culture. While God guides humanity through the Word and by the inspiration of the Spirit, God permits humanity to make decisions and to act either toward salvation (the reconciling of all things with God) or destruction (Josh 24:19–28; 1 Sam 8:4–22). Through both the rainbow following the flood (Gen

9:8–17) and the resurrection of Jesus (Mark 16:1–8), God promises to never, ever give up on humanity and the creation. God will never cease to draw humanity into the divinely conceived vision of intimate relationship with all things.

Who Is Jesus the Christ?

The cosmic Christ is the Light of day one of the creation and the Logos/Sophia of John 1 that precedes the creation ("all things came into being through him," John 1:3). This cosmic Christ was first incarnated through the creation and then again enfleshed in the person known as Jesus of Nazareth. Jesus the Christ stands as God's one-of-a-kind offspring (*monogenēs*, John 1:1–18), the prototype for humanity. In the person of Jesus, we discover what it means to be fully human, living in intimate relationship with God and with one another, serving and being generous to all. Jesus never self-identifies as the Christ/Messiah or King. God warned the people through Samuel (1 Sam 8:4–22) that they did not want a king/messiah, for God is our King. Jesus certainly is the Anointed One/Messiah, yet he does what every messiah/king prior to him should have done: die for his people and thus put an end to human hierarchy, division, isolation. He died so that all may live as one, serving God, humanity, and the creation. Through his resurrection, Jesus is the firstfruit of a new humanity created in love to draw all people into real life as new human beings who live truly as God-creatures committed to worship, relationships, service, and generosity.

What Is Sin?

The Greek word *hamartia* means "to miss the mark" in our humanity (Rom 5:12–14). Our focus is not on the predominant understanding of sin as breaking the law. Certainly, this is an aspect of sin. However, the more elegant understanding of sin is the human tendency to constantly break from our true identity as children of God and our true purpose to be the heart, hands, and feet of Jesus in the world. Sin produces evil and introduces hierarchy, division, violence, and animosity into the world, which destroys life (Gal 3:21–22).

Who Is the Holy Spirit?

The Holy Spirit, the Third Person of the Trinity, proceeds from the Father and the Son into the creation to work through humanity in drawing all things to God. The Spirit is the creative force of God, present in the creation from the beginning (Gen 1:1–2). The Spirit descended and remained on Jesus in his baptism by John (1:32–34) and then was transmitted by Jesus into the disciples to re-create them as new human beings to be sent to deliver the re-creating power of the Holy Spirit to others (John 20:22–23). We receive the Holy Spirit through baptism, in which we are put to death, drowned in the baptismal waters, and rebirthed as new human beings. We receive the Holy Spirit through the meal (Holy Communion), in which we're joined in intimate connection with God, one another, and the creation.

What Is the Church?

The church is the gathering of the new humanity (*ekklēsia*) "called out of" the world and rebirthed by Jesus through the power of the Holy Spirit (Rom 12; Eph 4:1–16). The church is an extension of the economic Trinity participating in the *missio Dei* to draw all things into relationship with God. We must fight against the common assertion that the church stands primarily as an institution. Rather, the church's true identity and purpose is as an organic, life-giving, Spirit-fueled movement in love for the sake of the world. All church functions and activities should be measured according to the *missio Dei*. The role of the church is to draw people into the new humanity, unleashing each for organic worship, relationships, service, and generosity so that all may experience real life in Jesus's name.

Holy Baptism

The Greek word *baptizō* literally means "to immerse, bathe, or wash." John the Baptizer called the people of Israel back to the Jordan River to be reimmersed in the water through which their Hebrew ancestors passed into the promised land. To understand John's activity, we must return to the Abrahamic covenant (Gen 12:1–3), in which God calls Abraham to trust God's three promises:

1. You will be the father of a great nation.

2. You and your family will have land on which to live.

3. All families/nations of the world will be blessed through you and your family.

At the time of the New Testament, the first two promises had been fulfilled, and yet the Hebrew people had forgotten the third promise, that they existed to be a blessing to all the world. John's call to baptism in the Jordan is a do-over of sorts to remind the people to return to their original identity and purpose. The Greek word for "repentance" in the text is *metanoia*, which means "a change of heart or mind." Jesus calls for the church to baptize (Matt 28:18–20) through immersion into water as a means of putting to death in us the old moral order of the world and rebirthing us purely as children of God, a return to our true identity and purpose. As baptized children of God, we are freed to live in intimate relationships with God and all humanity, seeing every person as a precious brother or sister, and working to build healing and reconciliation with all through love.

Holy Communion

If we understand the *missio Dei* as drawing all things into relationship with God, humanity, and creation, Holy Communion stands as the church's key vision for what this means. The eschatological feast of Isaiah 25:6–10a states that a day is coming when all will be gathered for a great feast celebrating intimate relationship to God and humanity. The word *all* is used five times in this passage to drive home the point that this vision is not about individual salvation (going to heaven after death) but a vision for the salvation of the world (bringing all things into oneness). When Jesus gathered with his disciples on the last evening before his death, he used the Passover meal (a story of liberation and new life) to enact the eschatological feast and to charge his followers to practice it whenever they can.

We see God's vision clearly through the meal, in that all who are gathered are invited to participate, thus representing the oneness of humanity. God is present through the word and promise that the body and blood of Christ are given and shed for you (plural). The creation is present through the sharing of the bread and wine. The pronouncement of "Christ's body and blood given and shed for you" carries multiple meanings. First, we hear the good news that we each are recipients of God's unconditional love and grace through the death and resurrection of Jesus the Christ. It's important that we recognize the "you" is plural, which again communicates that while this pronouncement is personal, it's not individual in nature. This pronouncement of good news in the meal connects us to God and one another. Also, the pronouncement of Christ's body and blood given and shed for you raises the question: What is the body of Christ? The church, as the restored community in oneness with God, is the body of Christ (Rom 7:4; 12:5; 1 Cor 12:12–31). Participation in the meal calls us as the body of Christ to be poured out for the sake of the world. God's vision of oneness with all is enacted in Holy Communion as a means for in-Spiriting us to be the body of Christ at home, work, school, neighborhood, and wherever we might find ourselves bringing reconciliation and new life to all.

What Is Salvation?

Salvation is to be understood as the culmination of the *missio Dei*, being drawn into relationship with God. The Greek word *sōzō*, which is often translated "to save," literally means to "be whole, well, or complete." The act of salvation is personal but not individual, meaning that while it involves persons, it is a corporate activity. Human wholeness and wellness depend on being re-membered, reconnected, and reconciled to God and to one another (Acts 2:43–47). Therefore, we cannot be saved without one another.

In What Can We Hope?

Hope is not wishful thinking. We often use the word *hope* to talk about things that we want to happen or to occur, but this is a misuse of the term. We have hope because we have a God who stands with us, never quits on us, and promises that life and love win. We have hope because we are surrounded by people who walk with us and encourage us. We have hope because we ourselves have the ability to act and do things that bring healing to ourselves and others. We have hope because we have countless blessings in our lives, and we get to be blessings in the lives of others. We don't generate hope within ourselves, but informed hope comes to us through the Jesus community to hold us as we face the challenges and adversities of life (Rom 5:1–5).

Trust versus Faith versus Belief

The Greek verb *pisteuō* can be translated as "trust," "having faith," or "believing." The terms *having faith* or *believing* in our culture today are largely held to mean a cognitive exercise in which we think something is real. We might ask someone, "Do you believe in ghosts?" or, "Do you believe in life on other planets?" or, "Do you believe in God?" "Trust" is the preferred translation of *pisteuō*, which then shifts the conversation from a cognitive exercise into a way of life. When we trust God, we align our lives accordingly, trusting that we have been claimed as children of God and called to be God's instruments of love and life as participants in the *missio Dei*. Trust is the foundation of every healthy relationship, and our trust in God and God's vision for humanity is the cornerstone in living our true identity as children of God.

Justice versus Righteousness

The Greek word *dikaiosynē* is often translated as "righteousness," which implies that our goal is to be in a "right relationship" with God. However, another and preferred translation of *dikaiosynē* is "justice." When we use this translation, we understand that we are called to be participants in executing God's justice in the world. God's justice is the unleashing of human beings to be everything that God created them to be, that is, new human beings who exist as children of God and who are unleashed to be the heart, hands, and feet of Jesus in the world. This understanding aligns with the *missio Dei* and leads to holistic, salvific action for the sake of the world versus an individualized self-focus on becoming "righteous" so that one can go to heaven after death.

Conclusion

Romans 1:16–17 is often mistranslated because it is co-opted by a hermeneutic lens built out of archaic doctrine or dogma. However, when we use the Abiding Hope hermeneutic, we find the passage to say something very different from what we read in either the New Revised Standard Version or New International Version of the Bible. Our translation reads:

> For I am not ashamed of the gospel [good news]; it is the power of God into salvation for all who are trusting, both Jew first and Gentile. For the justice of God in him has been disclosed out of trust into trust, just as it is written, "The just out of trust shall live." (Rom 1:16–17)

Paul places this passage early in his letter to the Romans to identify the life of Jesus as a fulfillment of the Abrahamic covenant. Paul asserts that Abraham trusted God so that through Abraham, God could actualize God's justice in the world and draw all people into relationship with God. Jesus, the one-of-a-kind offspring of both Abraham and God, also trusted God so that God could actualize justice through his life, death, and resurrection, which rebirths humanity to live fully as children of God. Now, we *all* are called *into* the trust of Jesus the Christ (called to trust God as Jesus trusted) so that through us, God will continue to actualize justice in the world.

To properly understand Paul's letters, we must comprehend this very important point. God is not interested in making people righteous so that they can go to heaven after they die. God is interested in drawing people into trusting relationships with God, as witnessed in the person of Jesus, so that through the new humanity, the Holy Spirit might create a human culture that produces justice and life for all. That, my friends, is the good news revealed through the life, death, and resurrection of Jesus. We as the church are blessed to be God's delivery system for bringing this good news to all the world.

Appendix C: Sample Accompaniment Covenant

Christ the King Lutheran Church, Denver, Colorado, Redevelopment Covenant

Preamble

Redevelopment is a process of biblical and spiritual renewal for individual members of Christ the King Lutheran Church as well as the congregation as a whole. Congregational redevelopment involves rerooting in the good news of Jesus Christ and getting God's dream for this ministry in focus. It is not a one-person project. It is God's project among us. It is not just about this congregation. It is about changing the world.

As such, we all have choices and commitments to make in living out God's dream for us. Because change is hard, as a congregation redevelops, it is essential that the partners share clear expectations and that accountability be strong. The partners of this redevelopment covenant are the pastors/redevelopment team, congregation, the Rocky Mountain Synod, and church-wide expressions of the ELCA. We hold this process in prayer, in hope that it will result in Christ the King Lutheran Church becoming a healthy, vibrant congregation.

Part One: Pastors/Redevelopment Team Call

In consultation with the Rocky Mountain Synod's office of the bishop, the congregation enters into relationship with Abiding Hope, Littleton, Colorado. During the years of redevelopment ministry, the director for evangelical mission and the Rocky Mountain Synod will accompany this process.

1. Christ the King agrees to enter into this covenant agreement with Abiding Hope until both parties concur that Christ the King is substantively positioned to return to being a fully autonomous, healthy, and thriving congregation.

2. Until such a time, the lead pastor and executive teams of Abiding Hope will serve as the mission redevelopers for Christ the King, Denver.

3. A guiding coalition will function as the congregational council/governing body for Christ the King, composed of an eight-member team: four members of Christ the King and three members of Abiding Hope along with the lead pastor (Doug Hill) of Abiding Hope. The director of evangelical mission for the Rocky Mountain Synod, Pastor Judith VanOsdol, will also be an ex officio part of the guiding coalition. The guiding coalition will strive to make all decisions by consensus and acclamation to lead the congregation with a sense of unity and purpose.

4. The four members of the guiding coalition from Christ the King will be selected through conversation with Christ the King council, Pastor VanOsdol, and Pastor Hill.

5. The guiding coalition will be responsible for
   - the vision and missional direction of the congregation,
   - all matters related to operations and finance,
   - the general health and vitality of the congregation.

6. Beyond the guiding coalition, congregation members will be invited and encouraged to serve in a variety of ministry settings (worship ministries, outreach initiatives, property and facility teams, etc.). Ministry teams will be equipped and supported to ensure that each ministry aligns with the overall vision and mission of the congregation.

7. Abiding Hope will supplement the ministry needs of Christ the King with Abiding Hope members until such time when Christ the King is able to support and maintain its ministries with servant leaders raised up from within the community.

8. All revenue collected in and through Christ the King will be invested in the vision and mission of the congregation. Abiding Hope will not receive, take, or keep any of the revenue originating from the Christ the King community. Abiding Hope will cover all expenses related to staff persons called to and employed by Abiding Hope. Christ the King will not be asked to reimburse or remunerate any expenses incurred by Abiding Hope during this covenant partnership. In the event of an employed staff person or other local initiative for Christ the King, such positions will be funded through Christ the King revenue and resources, subject to approval by the guiding coalition.

Appendix C

Part Two: Basic Expectations of the Pastors/ Redevelopment Team

Pastors are preachers and teachers, spiritual leaders, and evangelists. But a pastor/redevelopment team places a special emphasis on evangelism. The pastors/redevelopment team may organize a strategy to accomplish the following objectives of a normative redevelopment process:

1. Pray regularly, study Scripture, and listen to God's voice in leading the congregation.

2. Grow in discipleship and in personal financial stewardship and generosity (growth giving or tithing and beyond).

3. Be pastorally present for the people of Christ the King, including developing a plan for pastoral coverage, visitation, etc.

4. Develop, in a broad participatory process assisted by the director for evangelical mission, a three- to five-year vision for the congregation, with emphasis to include a plan for outreach, targeting a significant increase in worship attendance and making of disciples.

5. Include and equip others in leadership to use their gifts for God's mission.

6. Make creative use of all services of worship for the purpose of inviting new disciples, and lead in the adding of worship services as needed to maximize outreach.

7. Spend at least 50 percent of time in evangelizing outreach (including equipping laity for visiting sick/shut-

ins and others, for building relationships with and accompanying new disciples and growing in their ability to share their personal faith stories, and for cultivating a hospitable climate for growth).

8. Continue to learn and grow in evangelizing outreach skill through reading, workshops, and practice.

9. Regular communication that includes a process to assess and report regularly between the director of evangelical mission, redevelopment team, and congregation/community.

10. Actively participate in the life of the wider church, including synod assembly, theological conference, and conference gatherings and events.

11. During the redevelopment process, those portions of Christ the King's constitution related to congregational governance (council, structure, etc.) will be in suspension.

Part Three: Basic Expectations of the Congregation

Christ the King Lutheran Church commits itself to biblical and spiritual renewal, including intentional growth in worship attendance and financial support. The redevelopment team will communicate well and regularly, to cultivate a cooperative environment of shared leadership.

To fulfill the commitment, the congregation will:

1. Pray regularly, study Scripture, and listen to God's voice and dream for the congregation.

2. Grow in discipleship and in personal financial stewardship/generosity practices.

3. Install and support guiding coalition members, who strive to be a positive and visionary group rather than a negative and gatekeeping group, modeling transformation in the congregation.

4. Promote healthy, Christ-centered relationships and decision-making, refraining from gossip and negativity, and promote and embody a hopeful, missional attitude, living this out in words and actions.

5. Use God's gifts and find ways to engage the whole baptized people of God in ministry and outreach.

6. Be full partners in the task of evangelism: sharing faith and inviting people into ministry, and partnering in the tasks of visitation and follow-up.

7. Cultivate a climate of intentional hospitality for people new to life in the church.

8. Pray for and financially support evangelism/outreach activities in the community.

9. Change existing ministries and practices in order to live out God's dream more fully—with leadership provided by the pastors/redevelopers and the redevelopment team.

10. Support the interdependent work of the church by forwarding a percentage of all giving as mission support to the Rocky Mountain Synod, and develop a plan for growing that support each year (10 percent or more at end of three years).

11. Review and, if necessary, revise the current governing documents of the congregation.

12. Provide an atmosphere of trust and care, particularly for those in leadership.

13. Participate in the process of creating a three- to five-year vision for church growth with the redevelopment team and pastor/redeveloper.

14. Actively participate in the wider church, including the sending of two voting members to synod assembly yearly, and participate in conference gatherings.

Part Four: Basic Expectations of the Redevelopment Team

All redevelopments are a custom fit for each congregation, but the redevelopment of Christ the King Lutheran Church is unique: a hybrid where leadership is shared between the congregation and the redevelopment team that includes leaders from both Christ the King and Abiding Hope in Littleton, Colorado. The guiding coalition, as the redevelopment team, will communicate well, widely, and regularly within the congregation, to cultivate a cooperative environment of shared leadership.

Specifically, the guiding coalition/redevelopment team will:

1. As individual followers of Jesus, be models of the Christian life: regularly praying and studying Scripture, and practicing good, biblical financial stewardship (growth giving or tithing and beyond).

2. As congregational leaders, begin all meetings with worship or Bible study and prayer.

3. Work and communicate with the Rocky Mountain Synod director of evangelical mission, who will meet with the guiding coalition to help keep their work on track.

4. Foster a climate of goodwill, suppressing gossip and negativity in the congregation that would derail the mission of reaching out to the community with the good news of Jesus.

5. Promote and embody a hopeful, missional attitude, expressed in words and actions.

In addition, the redevelopment team will:

1. Create and guide a process of Bible study and discernment in the congregation, toward the goal of writing a statement of God's purpose for Christ the King Lutheran Church.

2. Create a three- to five-year vision and plan for outreach, increased worship attendance, and making of disciples, based on that purpose, with the redevelopment team and congregation.

3. Be a positive and visionary group rather than a negative and gatekeeping group, modeling transformation in the congregation.

4. Provide timely information to the congregation, including proposed redevelopment priorities and timeline.

5. Remain accessible to members and responsive to expressed concerns.

Part Five: Basic Expectations of the Office of the Bishop

On behalf of the Rocky Mountain Synod, the office of the bishop will support Christ the King Lutheran Church redevelopment efforts through the following:

1. Hold the process and its leaders and disciples in prayer, and communicate regularly.

2. Assist Christ the King Lutheran Church in procuring and promoting adequate leadership through partnership with Abiding Hope—to enable and empower redevelopment.

3. Meet with the guiding coalition monthly at first, then regularly.

4. Accompany the guiding coalition with prayer, leadership, and advocacy to discover God's vision for mission at Christ the King and its neighborhood and community.

5. Visit Christ the King Lutheran Church for Sunday worship and education.

Part Six: Considerations for the Outgoing Pastor of Christ the King

1. Christ the King will arrange a suitable farewell, recognition celebration, and "Godspeed" service, as well as provide a severance package for the outgoing pastor.

2. This package will include the continuation of the pastor and the pastor's family's Portico coverage for three months from the time of resignation or until the pastor receives another call, whichever comes first.

3. Should there be a time span greater than three months following the pastor's resignation before the pastor enters a new call, Abiding Hope will continue with the payments to Portico for both health and pension coverage for the pastor and the pastor's family for an additional three months, if necessary.

Appendix C

Part Seven: Term of the Covenant and Signatures

This covenant will form part of a discernment process with Christ the King beginning in June 2016 and brought before a vote of the entire congregation of Christ the King in July 2016. Should the Christ the King congregation vote favorably to accept the redevelopment relationship with Abiding Hope, the process and relationship would begin July 31, 2016, to be ratified by the Rocky Mountain Synod Council and be signed at the September 11 celebration of installation.

_____   _____
Partner Congregation Pastor (Print)   Signature/date

_____   _____
Partner Congregation Pastor (Print)   Signature/date

_____   _____
Abiding Hope Lead Pastor (Print)   Signature/date

_____   _____
Abiding Hope Congregation President (Print) Signature/date

_____   _____
Synod Director for Evangelical Mission (Print) Signature/date

_____   _____
Synod Council Vice President (Print)   Signature/date

_____   _____
Synod Bishop (Print)   Signature/date

_____ Date of Start of Partners

Acknowledgments

I am grateful to Fortress Press and its willingness to publish this book. I truly appreciate the support of Tim Blevins, CEO and president of 1517 Media, as well as Will Bergkamp, vice president and publisher for Fortress Press. I am particularly thankful for Fortress editor Scott Tunseth, for his incredible skills and expertise in converting my manuscript into this book. His wisdom and guidance have been a true blessing to me.

The one person who has played the most significant role in the creation of my manuscript is Stephanie Harper. She has been with me from start to finish, giving me advice for the chapter layout and flow, editing every sentence for clarity and consistency, and providing wisdom for how a manuscript becomes published. Without your help, I'm not sure this project would have been successfully completed. Steph, you are a true blessing to me! Sorry for all the commas.

It's critical that the readers know that much of what is in this book has been inspired and influenced by many others. Brad Binau at Trinity Lutheran Seminary served as my doctoral adviser and was an amazing coach in helping me to formulate my dissertation project, which has evolved into the concept of *Cultural Architecture*. Thank you, Brad, for your guidance, challenge, and partnership. Thank you to Herman Waetjen,

Matthew V. Johnson, and Jerry De Jesus for their incredible investment in me and the other doctoral candidates at San Francisco Theological Seminary. Each of them played a critical role in my formation of thinking that led to this book.

The person who has had the most impact on my formation is Rick Barger. Rick, thank you for serving as my mentor for nearly thirty years, for always having my back and being in my corner, for seeing more in me than I could see in myself, and for setting me on such strong theological and ecclesiological footing. I stand on your shoulders. You will undoubtedly hear your voice and see your fingerprints throughout this book.

I have deep appreciation for the amazing leaders and wonderful people of Abiding Hope Church, Littleton, CO, for being the heart, hands, and feet of Jesus in the world. Thank you for your continual investment in me and for giving me the time to study and write and to work with other congregations toward revitalization. Thank you also for your deep, deep passion for God's mission in the world. Your faithfulness, generosity, and spirit inspire me every single day. You are truly a wholly unleashed faith community.

And finally, thank you to Karrie, Sarah, and Jeremy, my precious family, for your constant love and support. There is no way that I would be able to do all that I do without you by my side. I have deep appreciation for your grace, encouragement, compassion, and commitment. You bless me each and every day and I thank God for you.